High School Spanish Review

THE PRINCETON REVIEW

High School
Spanish Review

BY ALEX IDAVOY

RANDOM HOUSE, INC.
www.randomhouse.com/princetonreview

Princeton Review Publishing, L.L.C.
2315 Broadway, 2nd Floor
New York, NY 10024
E-mail: comments@review.com

ISBN 0-375-75077-0

Editor: Lesly Atlas
Production Editor: Kristen Azzara
Production Coordinator: Evelin Sanchez-O'Hara

Manufactured in the United States of America on recycled paper.

9 8 7 6 5 4 3 2 1

First Edition

The Independent Education Consultants Association recognizes The Princeton Review as a valuable resource for high school and college students applying to college and graduate school.

DEDICATION

Dedico este libro a mis padres por haberme transmitido, además del español, su amor por Cuba.

I dedicate this book to my parents for having transmitted, in additon to Spanish, their love for Cuba.

ACKNOWLEDGMENTS

Thank you, Mario, for your generosity and advice all along the way. Thank you, Louisa, for your support and good humor. Thank you, Andres, for your technical assistance. And thank you, Lesly, for letting me take on my first book.

Special thanks to Dan Edmonds for his expert review of this project.

A very special thanks to Evelin Sanchez-O'Hara, Robert McCormack, Stephanie Martin, Jennifer Arias, Marika Alzadon, and Laurie Barnett for all of the extra effort they put into this project and especially for their patience. It is much appreciated!

CONTENTS

INTRODUCTION

Spanish is one of the most important languages in the world, spoken in over twenty different countries by more than 450 million people. Attempting to understand and become fluent in a foreign language entails understanding a culture, a history, and even a worldview.

Obviously, you can't become fluent by simply reading a book. But *High School Spanish Review* can lead you in the right direction! Here, at The Princeton Review, we support and encourage you in your attempt to conquer the language of *los conquistadores*. This review book presents the basics of Spanish that the average high school student covers in four years. Whether you're a high-school student seeking some extra help, a past student of Spanish who needs to resuscitate your language skills, a new-comer to the language, or a seasoned *profesor* or *profesora de Español, High School Spanish Review* will work for you.

The following chapters have been organized by communicative goals. What are you trying to achieve with the language? For example, do you want to ask a question? Tell a story? Give a command? You'll find that the grammar you need to reach your communicative goal is presented in as simple and entertaining a way as possible. Chapters are sprinkled with exercises that give you a chance to practice what we've just preached! Exercises go from the serious and traditional to the silly and outright politically incorrect. (Apologies ahead of time!) At the end of the book, we have included two practice exams option, as well as clear, helpful appendices as a reference.

I hope you enjoy my attempt to break down this code that took centuries to create! ¡VIVA EL ESPAÑOL!

Alex Idavoy, M.A.

1

Giving and Getting Information

Communication in any language usually consists of a series of questions and answers. Think about it. You are usually trying to get information or attempting to give it to someone else. What time is it? Time for you to learn Spanish. What's for dinner? Leftovers. Who writes the best review books? The Princeton Review, of course!

So let's start this review of Spanish by looking at how to formulate questions, and then from there we'll move on to answering them.

ASKING FOR INFORMATION
In Spanish you can ask a "yes" or "no" question by:

1. Raising the pitch of your voice at the end of a statement

2. Inverting the subject and verb

You can also use *question words* to get a specific type of information.

RAISING THE PITCH

El español es el idioma más interesante del mundo. Spanish is the most interesting langauge in the world. This is a declarative statement. But if we raise the pitch at the end of the statement, it becomes a question: *¿El español es el idioma más interesante del mundo?* Is Spanish the most interesting language in the world? The answer being: *¡Claro que sí!* Of course! (At least, according to the author of this book!)

EXERCISE 1.1

Look at the following statements. Practice reading them as questions by raising your intonation at the end of each sentence.

1. Hay muchos latinos en los Estados Unidos.

   There are many Latinos in the United States.

2. El español se habla mucho en Miami, Los Angeles, Chicago y Nueva York.

   Spanish is spoken a great deal in Miami, Los Angeles, Chicago and New York.

3. Para el año 2015, los hispanos serán el grupo minoritario más numeroso del país.

   By the year 2015, Hispanics will be the largest minority group in the United States.

INVERTING THE SUBJECT AND THE VERB

In the sentence: *¿Es el español el idioma más intersante del mundo?*, the verb *es* comes before its subject, *el español*. Look at this sentence: ¿Hablas bien el español? Do you speak Spanish well? Here the subject and verb are inverted, in a sense. The verb comes first, but the subject is not written, it is understood. If we were to include the subject, the question would read: *¿Hablas tú bien el español?* And it would mean exactly the same thing. While this will be covered further ahead, remember that the endings on the verbs indicate who is doing the action.

Questions that start with a verb are always "yes" or "no" questions. Take a look at the following questions. See what we mean?

> ¿Tienes (tú) las llaves del coche? Sí, yo tengo las llaves del coche.
>
> *Do you have the keys to the car? Yes, I have the keys to the car.*

¿Vives (tú) con la familia de Pedro? Sí, yo vivo con la familia de Pedro.

Do you live with Pedro's family? Yes, I live with Pedro's family.

¿Sabe el profesor dónde están los estudiantes? Sí, él sabe dónde están los estudiantes.

Does the professor know where the students are? Yes, he knows where the students are.

¿Tenemos (nosotros) suficiente dinero para la cena? No, no tenemos suficiente dinero para la cena.

Do we have enough money for dinner? No, we don't have enough money for dinner.

¿Comprenden ellos el sistema del metro? No, no comprenden el sistema del metro.

Do they understand the subway system? No, they don't understand the subway system.

EXERCISE 1.2

Answer the following questions about famous people.

1. ¿Habla Ricky Martin bien el español?

2 ¿Tiene Madona una hija que se llama Lourdes?

3 ¿Tiene Brad Pitt el pelo negro?

4. ¿Juega Michael Jordan bien al baloncesto?

Did you notice that all of the above questions called for "yes" or "no" answers? And that all the questions start with a verb?

QUESTION WORDS

To ask for specific types of information, as opposed to a simple yes or no answers, use the question words. Generally, the word order in this type of question is:

¿Question word + verb?

Note: The subject may or may not be written, but it will come *after* the verb. Remember we invert subject and verb when formulating questions.

Look at these examples:

¿Dónde?

¿Dónde está México, D.F. en este mapa? México está aquí.

Where is Mexico City on this map? Mexico City is here.

¿Adónde?

¿Adónde van Uds. para celebrar el año nuevo? A casa de mis tíos.

Where are you going to celebrate the New Year? To my aunt and uncle's house.

¿De dónde? (use to ask about place of origin)

¿De dónde es Antonio Banderas? España.

Where is Antonio Banderas from? Spain.

¿Qué?

¿Qué significa esta palabra? Esa palabra significa *esperanza*.

What does this word mean? That word means hope.

¿A qué hora?

¿A qué hora vino Carlos a buscarte anoche? ¡A las diez de la noche!

What time did Carlos come to pick you up last night? At ten o'clock at night!

¿Para qué?

¿Para qué se usa este programa? Para calcular las ventas.

What is this program used for? To calculate sales.

¿De qué color?

¿De qué color son los ojos de Jennifer López? Castaños.

What color are Jennifer Lopez's eyes? Brown.

¿Quién?

¿Quién tiene el boleto de Pablo? Lo tiene Pilar.

Who has Pablo's ticket? Pilar has it.

¿Quiénes?

¿Quiénes son estas personas en esta foto? Estos son mis compañeros de clase.

Who are these people in this picture? These are my classmates.

¿De quién?

¿De quién es esta bufanda? Es de Mercedes.

Whose scarf is this? It's Mercedes'.

¿Para quién?

¿Para quién son estos regalos? Para mis sobrinos, Tomás y Cristina.

Who are these gifts for? For my niece and nephew, Thomas and Christina.

¿Por qué?

¿Por qué siempre se me descompone el coche cuando más lo necesito? ¡Porque nunca le cambias el aceite, tonto!

Why does my car always break down when I need it most? Because you never change the oil, silly!

¿Cuándo?

¿Cuándo llegaron tus padres del Perú? El 23 de enero.

When did your parents arrive from Peru? On the 23rd of January.

¿Cuánto?

¿Cuánto vale esta camisa de seda? Mil pesos mexicanos.

How much is this silk shirt? One-thousand Mexican pesos.

¿Cuántos?

¿Cuántos niños hay en tu clase, Mario? Hay diez y ocho niños.

How many boys are there in your class, Mario? There are eighteen boys.

¿Cuánta?

¿Cuánta gasolina consume ese coche? ¡Demasiada!

How much gasoline does this car consume? Too much!

¿Cuántas?

¿Cuántas niñas hay en tu clase, MariCarmen? Quince niñas.

How many girls are there in your class, MariCarmen? Fifteen.

¿Cómo?

¿Cómo se llama tu novia? Patricia.

What is your girlfiend's name? Patricia.

¿Cómo + ser?

¿Cómo es La Habana? ¡Maravillosa!

What is Havana like? Marvelous!

¿Cómo + estar?

¿Cómo están tus padres? Están muy bien, gracias.

How are your parents? Very well, thanks.

¿Cuál?

¿Cuál es la respuesta correcta, A, B, C o D? ¡La respuesta correcta es C, por supuesto!

Which is the correct answer, A, B, C or D? The correct answer is C, of course!

¿Cuáles?

¿Cuáles son los libros para la clase de psicología? Estos.

Which are the books for the psychology class? These.

¿Cuál de? (this construction will be followed by a noun or pronoun)

¿Cuál de estas computadoras es la más rápida? *Gateway* es la más rápida.

Which of these computers is the fastest? Gateway is the fastest.

¿Cuáles de? (this construction will be followed by a noun or pronoun)

¿Cuáles de estos discos son argentinos? Los de tango, por supuesto.

Which of these records are Argentine? The tango ones, of course.

EXERCISE 1.3

Match the question words to their English translations. (Only the most common question words are included here.)

1. ¿Cómo?   A. How

2. ¿Cuánto?   B. What

3. ¿Cuándo?   C. When

4. ¿Dónde?   D. Where

5. ¿Por qué?   E. How much

6. ¿Qué?   F. Who

7. ¿Quién?   G. Why

EXERCISE 1.4

In the following dialogue, a young man named Emilio pays a visit to Miriam, his astrologer. He asks her a series of very specific questions. Look at the following questions, then at her answers. Try to fill in the question words based on Miriam's answers.

Emilio: Hola, Miriam.

Miriam: Hola, Emilio. ¿____1____ está Ud.?

Emilio: Bien. ¿Y Ud.?

Miriam: Muy bien, gracias. ¿Qué lo trae por aquí hoy?

Emilio: Hay algunas cosas que quisiera preguntarle.

Miriam: ¿Qué quiere saber exactamente?

Emilio: ¿____2____ se llama mi abuela?

Miriam: Su abuela se llama María Joséfina Villares del Mar de Villanueva.

Emilio: ¿____3____ vive ella?

Miriam: En Buenos Aires.

Emilio: ¿____4____ es la fecha de su cumpleaños?

Miriam: El 11 de mayo.

Emilio: ¿____5____ hermanos tiene ella?

Miriam: Ella tiene cuatro hermanos y tres hermanas.

Emilio: Muy bien. Ahora algunas preguntas sobre mi vida. ¿____6____ estuve yo en Puerto Rico?

Miriam: Estuviste en Puerto Rico en 1979.

Emilio: ¿____7____ es mi signo del horóscopo?

Miriam: Aries.

Emilio: ¿____8____ no tengo novia?

Miriam: Porque es un muchacho muy feo y antipático.

Emilio: ¿Qué? ¿____9____ cuesta su consulta?

Miriam: ¡Cien dólares!

EXERCISE 1.5

Read the following paragraph. Then complete the questions to the answers below.

> Miguel y Sofía salen de vacaciones en junio. Van a Bolivia, porque la familia de Miguel es de La Paz, la capital boliviana. El viaje es muy caro. Los boletos cuestan tres mil dólares. Miguel y Sofía son profesores en la Universidad de Miami.

1. ¿_____ salen de vacaciones? Miguel y Sofía.

2. ¿_____ salen de vacaciones? En junio.

3. ¿_____ van Miguel y Sofía de vacaciones? A La Paz, Bolivia.

4. ¿_____ es la familia de Miguel? Es de Bolivia.

5. ¿_____ cuestan los boletos? Tres mil dólares.

6. ¿_____ trabajan Miguel y Sofía? En la Universidad de Miami.

POINTING OUT PEOPLE, PLACES, AND THINGS

A noun represents a person, place, or thing. According to their meaning, nouns can be concrete (*un hombre, la casa, la maquina*) or abstract (*la moderación, la emoción, la democracia*). The Spanish word for noun is *sustantivo* (or *nombre*). Spanish nouns are either masculine or feminine, grammatically speaking. However, the meaning of a word does NOT determine its grammatical gender. Look at this example: *José es una persona inteligente.* (José is an intelligent person.) *Persona* is grammatically feminine, even though in this sentence it refers to a man.

Do not try to create your own rules to determine what makes a noun masculine or feminine—there is no logic to it. However, when you first learn a new noun, remember the definite article that accompanies it to help you remember whether the noun is masculine or feminine. Let's look at the nouns themselves first, then at the words connected to them, i.e., articles and adjectives.

The ending of a noun often indicates its gender.

Masculine Endings	Feminine Endings
-o (el zapato, el trabajo)	-a (la idea, la doctora)
-e (el café; el cliente)	-dad (la identidad, la cantidad)
-on (el buzón, el cinturón)	-tad (la libertad, la facultad)
-or (el terror; el pintor)	-z (la nariz, la actriz)
-án (el capitán, el caimán)	-sión, -ción (la explosión, la explicación)
-l (el papel, el hotel)	-umbre (la costumbre, la muchedumbre)
-s (el japonés, el interés)	
-r (el solar, el azar)	-ie (la especie, la serie)
-n (el jardín, el jazmín)	-ud (la virtud, la salud)

EXERICISE 1.6

Determine whether the following nouns are masculine or feminine based on the chart above. Fill in the blank before each of the following nouns, putting *el* in front of the masculine nouns and *la* in front of the feminine nouns.

1. biblioteca
2. casa
3. costumbre
4. cuidad
5. dolor
6. especie
7. guacamole
8. inspiración
9. interés
10. jardín
11. libertad
12. libro
13. Japón
14. papel
15. parque

While the majority of nouns follow this pattern, keep in mind that there are exceptions to these endings. For example, *agua* (water) and *problema* (problem) end in -a, but are masculine. *El agua, el problema.* Here some more exceptions:

el ataúd

el clima

el día

el drama

el mapa

el programa

el sistema

el telegrama

Mano (hand) is a feminine word ending in -*o*. *La mano.*

A few nouns may refer to either a man or a woman:

una persona

una víctima

un artista

To help you remember whether a noun is masculine or feminine, learn the article that accompanies it.

Indefinite articles are used to introduce a noun in a conversation or in a text.

Hay un ladrón en el patio.
There's a burglar in the yard.

He comprado un libro.
I bought a book.

Definite articles are used to refer to a specific noun.

La policía ha capturado al (a + el) ladrón.
The police captured the burglar.

El libro se titula "Cómo capturar ladrones."
The book is titled, "How to catch burglars."

Definite articles are also used when expressing a general truth.

> El sol brilla para todos.
> *The sun shines for everyone.*

> La vida es una gran escuela.
> *Life is a big school.*

Indefinite articles		Definite articles	
un libro	**unos** libros	**el** libro	**los** libros
una canción	**unas** canciones	**la** canción	**las** canciones

EXERCISE 1.7

Determine whether the followng nouns should be preceded by *el, la, los,* or *las.*

1. discotecas

2. especies

3. frustración

4. hijos

5. horrores

6. japonés

7. japonesa

8. libertades

9. mesas

10. muchedumbre

11. tamal

12. tapiz

13. terror

When used with a concrete noun, the definite article refers to a specific noun. The indefinite articles, on the other hand, do not refer to a noun specifically.

If you say *Quiero un coche* (I want a car), you're not referring to a specific car you want, but rather saying that *any* car will do. *Yo necesito un trabajo* (I need a job) doesn't specify which job you need; it just states that you need *any* job to pay the rent!

Look at these almost identical sentences.

> Mónica lleva un vestido azul.
>
> *Monica is wearing a blue dress.*

> Mónica lleva el vestido azul.
>
> *Monica is wearing the blue dress.*

CONTRACTIONS

When *el* is preceded by the preposition *a*, the two form the contraction *al*.

When *el* is preceded by the preposition *de*, the two form the contraction *del*.

The use of the contraction here has more to do with spoken than written Spanish. Since there are vowel sounds back to back, they blur into each other, and consequently are written in this abbreviated way.

La esposa del médico va al hospital del pueblo.

EXERCISE 1.8

Determine whether the followng sentences need to be rewritten to include the contractions.

1. Mis primos vienen a la fiesta de José.

2. Ellos van a conocer a el novio de María.

3. María es la dueña de la tienda.

4. Su familia es de el Ecuador.

5. José es de el Caribe, pero no sé de qué país.

TALKING ABOUT MORE THAN ONE

As you have probably figured out already, nouns in Spanish, like in English, are either singular or plural: *casa* (house) or *casas*, (houses). The formation of plurals is simple.

singular	plural
casa	casas
perro	perros
techo	techos
melón	melones
jamón	jamones

If the singular form of a noun ends in:	The plural ending is:
vowel	-s
consonant	-es
y	-es
z	-ces
és	-eses
án	-anes
ín	-ines
ón	-ones
én	-enes
e	-es

la casa	las casas
el español	los españoles
el rey	los reyes
el tapiz	los tapices
el francés	los franceses
el alemán	los alemanes
el jardín	los jardines
el jarrón	los jarrones
el fuerte	los fuertes
el examen	los exámenes
el mes	los meses
el dios	los dioses

EXERCISE 1.9

Write the plurals of the following nouns as well as their corresponding plural articles.

1. el libro   _____

2. una mesa   _____

3. la computadora   _____

4. un mesón   _____

5. un pollo   _____

6. una pared   _____

7. el español   _____

8. la española   _____

9. un juez   _____

10. el lápiz   _____

11. un coche   _____

12. un tapiz   _____

TALKING ABOUT ACTIONS

We've talked about nouns and articles. Now let's look at verbs, the most important part of a sentence. We'll get back to nouns, and adjectives, the words that describe them, later.

Expressing Existence: Hay

In Spanish, *hay* means *there is* when used with a singular noun, and *there are* when used with a plural noun.

¿Por qué hay un signo de interrogación aquí?
Why is there a question mark here?

¿Cuántos países hay en América Latina?
How many countires are there in Latin America?

Hay veinte.
There are twenty.

To say something does *not* exist, simply place "no" before *hay*.

> ¿Hay algún problema?
>
> No hay ningún problema.
>
> *Is there a problem?*
>
> *No, there's no problem.*

> ¿Hay empanadas frescas?
>
> No, no hay empanadas.
>
> *Are there fresh turnovers?*
>
> *No, there are no turnovers.*

PRESENT TENSE REGULAR VERBS

The infinitive is the most basic form of a verb. It is the form from which other forms are derived. All Spanish verbs end in *-ar, -er,* or *-ir.* For example: *hablar* (to dance), *comer* (to eat), and *vivir* (to live).

Depending on how verbs change when conjugated, they are either regular or irregular. Regular verbs follow a regular pattern. After memorizing one regular verb, you just have to apply the same pattern to other regular verbs. It would be nearly impossible to remember all the forms individually, for each verb has six forms in each tense and mood. Luckily the majority of the verbs are regular. Irregular verbs, then, are the verbs that don't follow a regular, predictable pattern. Some verbs are more irregular than others.

To talk about habitual actions in Spanish, we use the present indicative tense. The formation of a present indicative verb is easy. Regular verbs are verbs whose stems do not change; only the endings change.

Let's work with *bailar* (to dance). *Bailar* is a regular verb. Simply drop the *-ar* and add the following endings:

bailar — to dance

Singular	Plural
yo bail**o**	nosotros bail**amos**
tú bail**as**	vosotros bail**áis**
él/ella/Ud. bail**a**	ellos/ellas/Uds. bail**an**

The stem *bail-* is consistent throughout; only the endings change. This verb is regular in the present tense of the indicative mood.

Let's look at a regular -er verb:

comer — to eat

	Singular	Plural
	yo como	nosotros comemos
	tú comes	vosotros coméis
	él/ella/Ud. come	ellos/ellas/Uds. comen

And now a regular -ir verb:

vivir — to live

	Singular	Plural
	yo vivo	nosotros vivimos
	tú vives	vosotros vivís
	él/ella/Ud. vive	ellos/ellas/Uds. viven

STEM-CHANGING VERBS

The regular verbs you've seen so far are all consistent in their stems. In other words, their stems remain the same when conjugated. There are some verbs, however, whose stems change in the present. These are, of course, stem-changing verbs. Their endings are the same as the regular verbs.

There is a group of stem-changing verbs, where the *e* in the stem becomes *ie*:

cerrar — to close, to shut

	Singular	Plural
	yo cierro	nosotros cerramos
	tú cierras	vosotros cerráis
	él/ella/Ud. cierra	ellos/ellas/Uds. cierran

Notice that only the *yo*, *tú*, *él*, and *ellos* forms are affected. When you put the whole conjugation into two columns, the affected verbs form an L. One way to remember these forms is to think of these stem-changing verbs as "L" verbs. Some people also refer to them as "boot" verbs.

Other verbs that follow the same pattern as *cerrar*.

atraversar—to cross

comenzar—to begin

confesar—to confess

despertar—to awaken

despertarse—to wake up

empezar—to begin

encerrar—to enclose, to lock in

negar—to deny

pensar—to think, to plan

recomendar—to recommend

sentar—to seat

temblar—to tremble

Here's an example of a stem-changing *–er* verb:

encender — to light, to ignite

	Singular	Plural
	yo enciendo	nosotros encendemos
	tú enciendes	vosotros encendéis
	él/ella/Ud. enciende	ellos/ellas/Uds. encienden

Other verbs that follow the same pattern as *encender*.

defender—to defend

entender—to understand

querer—to want, to wish, to love (a person)

perder—to lose

Here's an example of a stem-changing *–ir* verb:

preferir — to prefer

	Singular	Plural
	yo prefiero	nosotros preferimos
	tú prefieres	vosotros preferís
	él/ella/Ud. prefiere	ellos/ellas/Uds. prefieren

Other verbs that follow the same pattern as *preferir*.

divertir—to amuse

divertirse—to enjoy oneself

mentir—to lie

sentir—to feel, to regret, to be sorry

sentirse—to feel (as in well, sick, etc.)

There is a group of stem-changing verbs, where the *o* becomes *ue*.

volver—to return

	Singular	Plural
	yo **vue**lvo	nosotros vo**l**vemos
	tú **vue**lves	vosotros vo**l**véis
	él/ella/Ud. **vue**lve	ellos/ellas/Uds. **vue**lven

Other verbs that follow the same pattern as *volver*:

acordarse (de)—to remember

acostar—to put to bed

acostarse—to go to bed, to lay down

almorzar—to have lunch

costar—to cost

contar—to count

demostrar—to demonstrate

encontrar—to find

encontrarse (con)—to meet

mostrar—to show

probar—to try, to taste

probarse—to try on

recordar—to remember

rogar—to beg

sonar—to sound, to ring

soñar—to dream

volar—to fly

delvover—to return, to give back

doler—to hurt; to ache

envolver—to wrap

llover—to rain

mover—to move

poder—to be able

There is a group of stem-changing verbs, where the *e* becomes *i*.

dormir — to sleep

Singular	Plural
yo duermo	nosotros dormimos
tú duermes	vosotros dormís
él/ella/Ud. duerme	ellos/ellas/Uds. duermen

pedir — to ask for

Singular	Plural
yo pido	nosotros pedimos
tú pides	vosotros pedís
él/ella/Ud. pide	ellos/ellas/Uds. piden

Other verbs that follow the same pattern as *pedir*:

conseguir—to get, to obtain

despedir—to fire (from a job)

despedirse—to say goodbye

medir—to measure

reír—to laugh

repetir—to repeat

seguir—to continue, to follow

servir—to serve

sonreír—to smile

vestir—to dress

vestirse—to get dressed

EXERCISE 1.10

Write out full sentences using the information provided.

1. José/jugar/bien/a el baloncesto.

2. Los vecinos/me/despertar/a las 6:00 de la mañana.

3. A veces/los alumnos/no entender/la lección.

4. En mi casa/nosotros/almorzar/a las 2:30 de la tarde.

5. ¿Cuánto/costar/el café?

6. Yo/no recordar/bien/la dirección.

7. ¿A qué hora/volver/tus padres?

8. Si yo no/dormir/suficientemente/no/poder/trabajar/mañana.

9. La dependiente/envolver/el regalo.

10. José/conseguir/buenos/precios/en/K-Mart.

REFLEXIVE VERBS

Verbs usually have direct objects, that is, nouns that are directly affected by their actions. When the direct object is the same as the subject, that is when the person that receives the action is the same person that did an action, we have a reflexive verb. Like a reflection in a mirror, reflexive verbs are verbs that come back to the subject.

Compare these two ideas:

> Yo baño al perro.
> *I bathe the dog.*

> Yo me baño.
> *I bathe myself.*

In the first sentence, "I bathe the dog," I am doing the action to the dog. The dog is affected by the action. In the second sentence, I do the action and receive the action as well. We have a reflexive verb. The infinitive form of the verb in the first sentence is *bañar*, but the infinitive of the second verb is *bañarse*. The *se* at the end of the infinitive indicates a reflexive verb.

Subject Pronouns	Reflexive Prounouns
yo	me
tú	te
él	se
ella	se
Ud.	se
nosotros	nos
vosotros	os
ellos	se
ellas	se
Uds.	se

When you learn reflexive pronouns (as well as direct and indirect object pronouns), memorize them in conjunction with the personal or subject pronouns. For example, while learning reflexive pronouns, study them as *yo/me, tú/te*, etc., don't just learn *me, te, se*, etc.

When ones says "John woke up," it's understood that John woke himself up. That is not the case in Spanish. If you say "Juan despertó," the implication is that he woke up someone else. The sentence is missing a direct object that tells who he woke up. The reflexive verb, *despertarse*, on the other hand, means the subject will do the action onto itself. *Juan se despertó*. Juan woke himself up.

EXERCISE 1.11

Look at the following illustrations about Maria's daily routine. Put the statements in order according to the pictures.

1. Ella se baña rápidamente.

2. Se desayuna café con leche y pan tostado.

3. Se pone un poco de maquillaje en la cara.

4. Se pone su perfume preferido.

5. Se seca el cuerpo con una toalla.

6. Se pone la ropa.

7. Se acuesta a las 10 de la noche.

8. Se levanta a las 7 de la mañana.

9. Se despierta a las 6:30 de la mañana.

10. Se prepara una cena saludable.

Other reflexive verbs:

asustarse—to get afraid, to get scared

aburrirse—to get/become bored

casare—to get married

cansarse—to get/become tired

desmayarse—to faint

enfadarse—to get/become angry

resfriarse—to get a cold, to catch a cold

mojarse—to get wet

levantarse—to get up (out of bed)

desayunarse—to have breakfast

vestirse—to get dressed

ponerse la ropa—to get dressed (literally, to put on clothes)

quitarse la ropa—to get undressed (literally to take off clothes)

acostarse—to lay oneself down; to go to sleep

acordarse—to remember

apresurarse—to hurry

arrepentirse—to regret

atreverse a—to dare to

burlarse de—to mock; to make fun of

negarse a—to refuse to

olvidarse de—to forget about

parecerse a—to resemble; to look like

quejarse—to complain

reirse de—to laugh at

tratarse de—to be concerned with, to be about (as in an article)

RECIPROCAL VERBS

In the following sentences, the subjects do the actions to each other.

Ellos **se quieren** mucho.
They love each other very much.

Nos vemos todos los días.
We see each other everyday.

Ellos **se saludaron** muy formalmente.
They greeted each other very formally.

Los hombres **se dan la mano**, pero las mujeres se besan.
Men shake each other's hands, but women kiss (each other).

Notice that the sentences are all plural and that the reflexive pronouns refer back to the subjects. That's what makes them reciprocal.

The context of a sentence tells you whether the verb is reflexive or reciprical.

Reflexive (myself)	Reciprocal (each other)
Yo me miro en el espejo.	**Ellos se miraron** intensamente.
I look at myself in the mirror.	They look at each other intensely.

Some common reciprocal verbs:

abrazarse—to hug

besarse—to kiss

comprenderse—to understand

conocerse—to know

darse la mano—to shake hands

divorciarse—to divorce

casarse—to marry

mirarse—to look

parecerse—to look like

quererse—to love

reconocerse—to recognize

respetarse—to respect

verse—to see

odiarse—to hate

THE IMPERSONAL *SE*

The *impersonal se* in Spanish is the equivalent of the impersonal you, one, they, or the passive construction in English. These sentences do not refer to anyone in particular, making them impersonal.

You can never say never.
One can never be too careful.
Fine wines are sold here.

Look at the translations of the English sentences above.

Nunca se puede decir nunca.
Nunca se puede ser demasiado cuidadoso.

Se venden vinos* finos aquí.

*If the topic of the sentence is plural, the verb usually is, as well.

Se esperan muchos refugiados políticos este año.
They expect a lot of politcal refugees this year.

Se vende esta casa.
They are selling this house.

EXERCISE 1.12

Imagine that you work for a newspaper. Write the headings for different advertisements and classified ads using the information given.

EXAMPLE: ofrecer/mejor/precios

Se ofrecen los mejores precios.

1. vender/casa/grande

2. comprar/camaras/de segunda mano (second-hand)

3. buscar/profesora/español

4. alquilar/habitación en apartamento céntrico

5. traducir/documentos/oficiales

Se + third person singular form may also be used for instruction, for example in a recipe.

Se ponen los tomates en un sartén.
You put the tomatoes in a frying pan.

Se fríen las patatas.
You fry the potatoes.

Se baten los huevos.
You beat the eggs.

EXPRESSIONS WITH INFINITIVES

There are many expressions that require the infinitive. In these, the first verb is conjugated, and the second is left in the infinitive form.

Yo quiero vivir en España.
I want to live in Spain.

El abogado necesita hablar con su cliente.
The lawyer needs to speak to his client.

For the sake of organization, let's take a look at these expressions by meaning.

EXPRESSING DUTY AND OBLIGATION

These expressions are used to express obligation.

tener que—to have to

deber—should, ought to

necesitar—to need

hay que—one must

es necesario—it is necessary

Tenemos que pagar impuestos.
We have to pay taxes.

Los estudiantes deben entregar sus cuadernos a tiempo.
The students should hand in their workbooks on time.

Necesito comer desayuno.
I need to eat breakfast.

Hay que mantener un saldo de por lo menos cien dólares.
One must maintain a balance of at least one-hundred dollars.

Es necesario tomar vitaminas.
It is necessary to take vitamins.

To use these expressions, you must conjugate the first verb. *Hay que* and *es necesario,* however, are impersonal expressions and are *not* conguated.

TO EXPRESS PREFERENCE AND DESIRE

The next group is used to express preference and desire.

preferir—to prefer

querer—to want

tener ganas de—to feel like (doing something)

Prefiero manejar un coche de cambios.
I prefer to drive a stick-shift car.

Quiero comprar un Toyota de cambios.
I want to buy a stick-shift Toyota.

Tengo ganas de comer una hamburguesa.
I feel like eating a hamburger.

Expressing Plans and Intentions: *pensar, quisiera, me gustaría*

Yo pienso tomar mis vacaciones en mayo este año.
I'm thinking about taking my vacation in May this year.

Yo quisiera viajar a Turquía este año.
I would like to travel to Turkey this year.

Me gustaría pasar dos semanas en Estambul.
I would like to spend two weeks in Istanbul.

Expressing likes and dislikes: *gustar, encantar*
To say that you like to do something, use *gustar + infinitive. Gustar* means to like, or to be pleasing to someone.

Me gusta nadar.
I like to swim.
Swimming is pleasing to me.

Gustar is used with the indirect object pronouns that tell to whom an activity is pleasing.

Singular	Plural
me — *to me*	**nos** — *to us*
te — *to you, to him, to her*	**os** — *to you*
le — *to you (polite, singular)*	**les** — *to you, to them (polite, plural)*

Me gusta manejar.
I like to drive.

¿Te gusta patinar?
Do you like to skate?

Le gusta estudiar.
She likes to study.

Nos gusta comer en ese restaurante.
We like to eat in that restaurant.

¿Os gusta salir a bailar?
You like to go out dancing?

Les gusta viajar.
They like to travel.

Since *le gusta* can mean either "he likes," "she likes," or "you like" and *les gusta* can mean "they like," or "you (pl.) like," Spanish speakers commonly add a pronoun or a noun to indicate who is being referred to.

A él le gusta viajar
He likes to travel.

A ella le gusta esquiar en Chile.
She likes to ski in Chile.

A Mario le gusta estudiar árabe.
Mario likes to study Arabic.

A Uds. les gusta ir de copas.
You (pl) like to go out drinking.

A ellos les gusta montar en bicicleta.
They (masc.) like to go bike riding.

A ellas les gusta tocar la guitarra.
They (fem.) like to play the guitar.

A Elena y a Martin les gusta comer en casa.
Elena and Martin like to eat at home.

Others verbs like *gustar*

dar miedo—to frighten

dar rabia—to anger

fascinar—to love

interesar—to be interesting

llamar la atención—to attract attention

molestar—to bother

parecer—to seem like

preocupar—to worry

urgir—to be pressing

> Nos da miedo estar solos en esta casa.
> *It frightens us to be alone in this house.*

> Me da rabia ver a ese hombre.
> *It infuriates me to see that man.*

> A mis hijos les fascina ir a Nueva York.
> *My children love to go to New York.*

Ordering events: *después de y antes de*

Después de and *antes de* are prepositions that are followed by the infitive when talking about the order of action.

> Yo me baño antes de desayunar.
> *I take a shower before I have breakast.*

> Yo desayuno después de bañarme.
> *I have breakfast after I take a shower.*

Is the Glass Half Full or Half Empty?

algo—something	nada—nothing
alguien—someone	nadie—nobody
algún—some	ningún—none, no one
alguno/a/os/as—some, any	ninguno/a/de—none of
siempre—always	nunca—never
también—also	tampoco—neither

Seremos libres algún día.
We'll be free some day.

Hemos tomado algunas medidas importantes.
We have taken some important steps.

Doctor, ¿tenemos alguna esperanza de que se recupere?
Doctor, do we have any hope for his recovery?

Sí, hay algunos medicamentos muy eficaces.
Yes, there are some very effective drugs.

Ningún hombre
No man

Ningunos hombres
No men

Ninguna idea
No idea

Ningunas ideas
No ideas

Double negatives are used often in Spanish.

¿Hay algo intersante aquí?
Is there anything interesting here?

No, no hay nada interesante.
No, there's nothing interesting.

¿Tienes algo para mi?
Do you have something for me?

No, no tengo nada.
No, I have nothing for you.

¿Pilar, siempre viajas en la aerolínea *Continental* cuando vas a Colombia?
Pilar, do you always travel on Continental Airlines when you go to Colombia?

No, nunca tomo *Continental*. Prefiero *Avianca*.
No, I never take Continental. I prefer Avianca.

¿Hay algunos estudiantes sin libros?
Are there any students without books?

No, no hay ningún estudiante sin libros.
No, there are no students without books.

¿Hay alguna doctora presente?
Is there a doctor in the house?

No, no hay ninguna.
No, there isn't one.

Alguno and *ninguno* become *algún* and *ningún* before masculine singular nouns.

¿Cononces tú algún restaurante peruano en esta zona?
Do you know of a Peruvian restaurant in this area?

No is not used when the negative comes before the verb.

Nunca tengo que trabajar los sábados.
I never have to work on Saturdays.

¡Nadie me ayudó!
Nobody helped me!

To express the idea of "me neither, "you neither," and so on, use the subject pronoun + *tampoco*.

No quiero ser su compañero de cuarto.
I don't want to be his/her roommate.

Yo tampoco.
Me neither/I don't either

Yo no confío en la globalización. Tú tampoco, ¿verdad?
I do not trust globalization. You don't either, do you?

EXERCISE 1.13

Answer the following questions negatively. Use *nada, nadie, nunca, o ninguno/a*.

Example: ¿Hay algo de beber en el refrigerador?
No, no hay nada.

1. ¿Supiste algo de José.

   No, no supe _____.

2. ¿Alguien estuvo en mi habitación anoche?

   No, _____.

3. ¿Siempre fumas cigarillos Marlboro cuando tomas café cubano?

   _____ fumo Marlboro. Prefiero Winston.

4. ¿Me compraste una camisa nueva?

   Lo siento, pero no encontré _____ bonita.

5. ¿Por qué no invitaste a María y a José a mi fiesta?

   Los invité, pero _____ de los dos me respondió.

TALKING ABOUT ACTIONS IN PROGRESS

PRESENT PROGRESSIVE

To talk about what is going on *at this moment*, there is a special construction, similar to English. This is called the present progressive, *el presente progresivo*. In English, we use the present progressive to talk about what we are doing at the moment, but also over a period of time. "I am taking a great Spanish course. I'm reading a great book on Spanish." In Spanish, you would use the present indicative for these sentences. *"Estudio español este semestre. Leo un libro muy intersante acerca del español."*

The present progressive in Spanish refers to what is happening at the moment. To form the present progressive is easy! Simply conjugate *estar* and tack on the present participle.

To form the present participle in *-ar* verbs, drop the *-ar* ending and add *-ando* to the stem.

hablar—habl—hablando

For -er and -ir verbs, add -iendo to the stem.

comer—com—comiendo

vivir—viv—viviendo

Participles do not change according to the number or gender of the subject.

El está trabajando.

Ellas están trabajando.

Since participles don't change according to the subject, they are NOT conjugated verbs.

Some irregular present participles to watch out for

decir—diciendo

divertirse—divirtiendo

dormir—durmiendo

pedir—pidiendo

servir—sirviendo

mentir—mintiendo

reír—riendo

leer—leyendo

caer—cayendo

traer—trayendo

oír—oyendo

Subject	Estar conjugated	Present participle
yo	estoy	estudiando español
tú	estás	escribiéndole una carta a José
él	está	llamando a su novia
ella	está	pensando en su novio
Ud.	está	leyendo este libro
nosotros	estamos	esperando el autobús
vosotros	estáis	trabajando mucho
ellos	están	revisando las composiciones
ellas	están	subiendo las escaleras
Uds.	están	mirando la tele

EXERCISE 1.14

José and María are on vacation. They are at the poolside and speculate about what their pets are probably up to at this moment. Write
the present progressive form of the indicated verbs.

1. El perro _____ (jugar) con mis zapatillas.

2. El gato _____ (arañar) la madera de las puertas.

3. El loro _____ (hablar) sin parar.

4. Los ratones _____ (subirse) al mostrador de
la cocina.

5. Los canarios _____ (cantar).

EXERCISE 1.15

Write the present progressive form of the indicated verbs.

1. José y María _____ (dormir) en la alcoba
de arriba.

2. El mesero _____ (servir) a los Ramírez.

3. ¿Cómo se llama el libro que _____ (leer)
tú?

4. ¿Por qué _____ (reírse)* tanto Uds.?

5. ¿Qué me _____ (decir) él? No
entiendo inglés.

*When using an object pronoun or a reflexive pronoun with the
present progressive, the pronoun can be placed before *estar* or attached to the end of the present participle.

El se está bañando = El está bañándose.

El me está explicando la lección = El está explicándomela.

WORDS THAT DESCRIBE

Adjectives are used to describe nouns.

Article	Noun	Adjective
la	casa	blanca
el	carro	rojo
una	idea	genial
un	hombre	alto

An adjective must agree in gender and number with the noun it describes. If the noun is masculine and singular, i.e., *el señor*, the adjective(s) that describe it must also be masculine and singular: *El señor tímido.*

If the noun is feminine and singular, the adjective must agree, or be feminine and singular, as well: *La señora tímida.*

And if the noun is masculine and plural, its corresponding adjective must be as well: *Los señores tímidos.*

With feminine and plural nouns, the adjectives follow suit: *Las señoras tímidas.*

To determine the correct form of the adjective, analyze the noun it is describing. This is why knowing the gender of the nouns you use is so important.

Adjectives that end in *-o* are masculine and those that end in *-a* are feminine.

> Miguel es creativo.
> María es creativa.

The rules for forming the plural of adjectives are the same as for nouns. (See page 13.)

EXERCISE 1.16

Give the opposite gender of the following adjectives.

1. introvertido _____

2. organizada _____

3. simpático _____

4. atlética _____

5. reservado _____

There are some adjectives that are the same in both the masculine and feminine forms.

Juan es popular.

María es popular.

El niño es obediente.

La niña es obediente.

Other examples:

interesante

amable

idealista

intelectual

cruel

EXERCISE 1.17

Match the following nouns to the most appropriate adjectives.

Note: You do NOT need to know what the words mean. Use your knowledge of noun/adjective agreement.

1. la leche (milk)   A simpáticas

2. los hermanos (siblings)   B italiano

3. las niñas (girls)   C cremosa

4. el estudiante (student)   D generosos

TALKING ABOUT NATIONALITY

A specific type of adjective is nationality. When you say Charles is British, you are describing Charles by referring specifically to his country of origin or, in some cases, his cultural identity.

To form the feminine of most nationalities, just add -a to the masculine form.	
español	española
portugués	portuguesa
alemán	alemana
francés	francesa

With other nationalities, the masculine ends in -o and the feminine in -a.

italiano	italiana
chino	china
polaco	polaca
mexicano	mexicana

Additional nationalities are listed in the appendix.

EXERCISE 1.18

Determine whether the noun being described requires the masculine or feminine form of the nationality indicated by the country given.

1. Roman Polanski es de Polonia; él es _____.

2. La familia de Madona es de Italia; su familia es _____.

3. París es la capital de Francia; es la capital _____.

4. Me gusta el vino de España; me gusta el vino _____.

5. Ricky Martin es de Puerto Rico; él es _____ .

6. Los padres de Jennifer López son de Puerto Rico; ellos son

    _____.

7. Andy García es de Cuba; él es _____.

8. Glora Estefan es de Cuba; ella es _____.

NOTE: Nationalities are lower case in Spanish, unlike in English.
Fidel Castro es cubano. Bill Clinton es estadounidense.

PLACEMENT OF ADJECTIVES

As you may have noted, in Spanish, adjectives come *after* the noun they describe. For example, English speakers would say that the U.S. president lives in the White House; a Spanish speaker would call the presidential dwelling '*La Casa Blanca.*' This is the case with the vast majority of adjectives in Spanish.

There are cases where it is appropriate to put the adjective first, but they are rare. The placement of an adjective, however, can affect its meaning. For example, if you say, *el hombre pobre*, that means the poor man, who has no income. But *el pobre hombre*, means the poor, pitiful man who has had hard luck. At this point, assume that the adjective comes *after* the noun it describes.

Adjectives that describe usually come after the noun. The following adjectives change a bit when placed BEFORE the noun they describe.

These masculine adjectives all drop the final *o*: *bueno, malo, primero, tercero*.

un hombre **bueno**	un **buen** hombre
un hombre **malo**	un **mal** hombre

Grande becomes *gran* before a singular noun.

el Río **Grande**	el **gran** río

COGNATES

There are many words in Spanish whose meaning is easy for an English speaker to decipher because of its similarity to English. Words that have similar or identical spellings and the same meaning in both languages are called *cognates*. Cognates are important to recognize. They will come in very handy, whether you're reading, writing, listening, or speaking. They are especially, helpful, however, in reading.

Take a wild guess as to the meaning of these Spanish cognates:

agresivo

mágico

terrible

indestructible

fantástico

EXERCISE 1.19

Try to match the list of cognates to the activities below. Column A is a list of adjectives describing José. Which activities in Column B would seem most logically related to each adjective?

For example, *José es atlético; el juega bien al fútbol y al tenis.*

Column A

    José es

1. cruel

2. extrovertido

3. franco

4. intelectual

5. inteligente

6. reservado

7. sentimental

8. tímido

Column B

a) abusa de los animales pequeños, como los gatitos

b) dice exactamente lo que piensa

c) entiende avanzados conceptos matemáticos

d) habla mucho de sus ideas políticas y filosóficas

e) hace los papeles principales en las obras de teatro en la escuela

f) llora mucho cuando ve las películas románticas

g) no habla mucho de su vida privada

h) se le pone roja la cara cuando le hablan

Look for these correlations to help you recognize cognates in your readings.

If a word ends with	The English equivalent would be
-ar	-ate
-ción	-tion
-dad	-ty
-ía	-y
-io	-e
-mente	-ly
-oso	-ous

EXERCISE 1.20

What are the English cognates for the following Spanish words?

1. explicación

2. posiblemente

3. biología

4. fraternidad

5. participar

POINTING THINGS (AND PEOPLE AND PLACES) OUT: *DEMONSTRATIVE ADJECTIVES*

Demonstrative pronouns point out specific nouns, be they people, places, things, ideas, etc.

Masculine		Feminine		
singular	**plural**	**singular**	**plural**	
este	estos	esta	estas	*this, these*
ese	esos	esa	esas	*that, those*
aquel	aquellos	aquella	aquellas	*that, those (over there)*

To figure out which demonstrative pronoun you need:

1. Determine where the specific thing is.

   A. Is it close to you, the speaker?

   Este teléfono no funciona.

   This telephone doesn't work.

   B. Is it close to the listener?

   Ese teléfono está roto.

   That telephone is broken.

   C. Or is it far from both the speaker and the listener?

   Aquel teléfono funciona bien.

   That telephone (over there) works well.

2. Determine whether the specific noun is masculine or feminine, singular or plural. Demonstrative adjectives must agree in both gender and number with the noun they are pointing out. They always come BEFORE the noun they are describing.

Use the following if the noun is		
close to speaker	**close to listener**	**far from both**
este — *this*	ese — *that*	aquel — *that (over there)*
esta — *this*	esa — *that*	aquellos — *that (over there)*
estos — *these*	esos — *those*	aquella — *those (over there)*
estas — *these*	esas — *those*	aquellas — *those (over there)*

Esta blusa me queda bien.
This blouse fits me well.

Esa blusa te queda bien.
That blouse fits you well.

Aquella blusa es muy elegante.
That blouse (over there) is very elegant.

Look at this sentence.

Esa camisa combina mejor con estos pantalones.
That shirt matches these pants better.

Camisa is feminine and singular, so we use *esa* to point it out. *Pantalones*, on the other hand, is masculine and plural, so we use *estos* to point them out.

EXPRESSING POSSESSION

There are various ways to express possession in Spanish:

de + person:	Los libros *de Marta*.
possessive adjectives:	Este es *mi* libro.
possessive pronouns:	Este libro es *suyo*.
the verb *tener*:	La biblioteca *tiene* muchos libros.

DE + PERSON

El novio de María es argentino. If we were to translate literally, this sentence reads: "The boyfriend of María is Argentine." But of course, we would say: "María's boyfriend is Argentine."

La bandarea de México es verde, roja y blanca.

Los estudiantes de la Universidad Autónoma de México son excelentes.

En la capital de México hay mucha contaminación ambiental.

La colección del Museo de Antropología es excepcional.

POSSESSIVE ADJECTIVES

Possessive adjectives are words that describe nouns by indicating possession.

EXERCISE 1.21

Look the following sentences. Each one contains a different possessive adjective. Find the possessive adjectives.

1. Esta es mi casa.

2. ¿Es tu hermano mayor o menor?

3. Antonio Banderas vive con su esposa, Melanie Griffith.

4. Mi novia y yo tenemos nuestros problemas.

5. ¿Están listas vuestras hijas?

6. Las mujeres bailan con sus esposos.

POSSESIVE PRONOUNS

Like in English, pronouns can indicate possession. The possessive pronouns take the place of a noun and also indicate the owner of that noun. Pronouns must agree in gender and number with the nouns they are replacing.

Esta computadora es mía. *Mía* is in the feminine, singular form because it is referring to *computadora*, which is also feminine and singular.

Look at this sentence: *Estas computadoras son mías.* We keep *mí.* The -*as* indiciates a possessive pronoun and refers to a feminine, plural noun, in this case, *computadoras.*

Possessive Pronouns	
mío/a/os/as	mine
tuyo/a/os/as	your
suyo/a/os/as	his, hers, your (formal)
nuestro/a/os/as	our
vuestro/a/os/as	your
suyo/a/os/as	their

THE VERB *TENER* TO SHOW POSSESSION

Tener simply means to have. It is commonly used to show possession.
Examples:

Tengo un Mercedes-Benz.

Carlos tiene mi dinero.

Nosotros tenemos un chateau en Francia.

TO BE OR TO BE: IS IT *SER* OR *ESTAR*?

Spanish is one of the few languages that has two verbs that mean "to
be": *ser* and *estar*. So, when do you use one or the other? Before we
get to that, take a look at how they are conjugated in the present.

Ser	Estar
Soy filipino.	**Estoy** en Manila
¿Eres de Jamaica?	**¿Estás** de visita?
Es excelente mecánico.	**Está** en el taller.
Somos esbeltas.	**Estamos** haciendo ejercicios.
¿Sois demócratas?	**¿Estáis** de acuerdo con la plataforma?
Son rojos.	**Están** verdes.

Basically, *ser* refers to the *permanent* or *inherent* qualities, as opposed
to *estar*, which is used to describe *transient* or *temporary* states.

Look at the following passage. Try to determine from the context
just how *ser* is used.

María *es* colombiana. Ella *es* de Cartagena, Colombia. Ella *es*
dentista. *Es* alta. Ella *es* amable.

Ser is used to indicate:

Nationality/origin	Profession/occupation	Physical traits/personality traits
María *es* colombiana.	*Es* dentista.	*Es* alta. *Es* amable.
María is Colombian.	*She is a dentist.*	*She is tall. She is friendly.*
Es de Colombia.		
She is from Colombia.		

Ser is also used to tell time and give dates.

¿Qué hora es?

What time is it?

Son las siete y media.

It's 7:30.

¿Qué hora es?

What time is it?

Es la una.

It's one.

The one o'clock hour takes the third person singular of *ser*. The others take the plural.

Hoy es 26 de marzo.

Today is the 26th of March.

Ser + de is also used to express possession.

¿Este anillo es de tu abuela?

Is this ring your grandmother's?

Sí, y estos collares son de ella, también.

Yes, and these necklaces are hers, too.

ESTAR

Now look at this short passage with *estar*.

Elena *está* muy enferma. Ella *está* en el hospital.

Estar is used to refer to:

Physical states	Mental states	Location
Elena *está* muy enferma.	Ella *está* muy nerviosa.	Ella *está* en el hospital.
Elena is very sick	She is very nervous	She is in the hospital

Estar used to express physical and mental states, as well as location, will be covered just ahead.

ADJECTIVES WITH *SER* VS. *ESTAR*

As if there weren't enough to deal with already, certain adjectives change their meanings if used with *ser* or *estar*.

Look at these examples:

>Eres interesado.
>
>*You are egotistical.*

>Estás interesado.
>
>*You are interested.*

>Silvia es delicada.
>
>*Silvia is a delicate person.*

>Silvia está delicada.
>
>*Silvia's health is frail.*

>Felipe es malo.
>
>*Felipe is a bad person.*

>Felipe está malo.
>
>*Felipe is sick.*

THE PASSIVE VOICE: *SER* VS. *ESTAR* + PAST PARTICIPLES

Ser + past participle expresses the passive voice in Spanish. It's not used as often as it is in English, but it is worth noting.

>La Internet **es usada** por millones de personas.
>
>*The Internet is used by millions of people.*

>El candidato **es apoyado** por los votantes.
>
>*The candidate is supported by the voters.*

>La policía **no es respetada** en este barrio.
>
>*The police are not respected in this neighborhood.*

Estar + past participle is used to express a condition resulting from an action. Not as complicated as it sounds! With these constructions, however, the "doer" of the action is never mentioned.

La tienda está abierta.

The store is open. (the result of someone opening it!)

The "someone" who opened the store is implied.

Los niños ya están sentados.

The children are already seated.

Who sat them? We don't know.

TALKING ABOUT LOCATION

Both *ser* and *estar* are used in connection to location, but in different ways.

Estar is used to give the location of people or things.

¿Dónde está Karina?

Where's Karina?

Karina está en su cuarto.

Karina is in her room.

¿Dónde está Quito?

Where's Quito?

Quito está en el Ecuador.

Quito is in Ecuador.

Ser is used to tell the location of an event.

¿Dónde es la fiesta?

Where is the party?

La fiesta es en la casa de Luisa.

The party is at Luisa's house.

¿Dónde son las reuniones normalmente?

Where are the meetings normally?

En el segundo piso.

On the second floor.

TALKING ABOUT MENTAL AND PHYSICAL STATES

Estar is also used to talk about temporary mental and physical states. Look at the illustrations in the following exercise and then try to match up their meanings.

EXERCISE 1.22

1. estar apurado

2. estar cansado

3. estar de buen humor

4. estar de mal humor

5. estar enojado

6. estar nervioso

AGREEMENT

When we discuss physical and mental states, *estar* has to be conjugated AND the adjective must agree in gender and number with the subject.

José está enojado.

Jose is angry.

María está enojada.

Maria is angry.

Mis hermanos no están enojados.

My brothers are not angry.

Nosotras estamos enojadas.

We are angry.

For example, since José is masculine and singular, the adjective *enojado* is also masculine and singular. María is feminine and singular, and so the feminine and singular *enojada* is used. The same applies for the plural forms.

MORE PHYSICAL AND MENTAL STATES

The following mental and physical states are constructed just a bit differently than the ones above. Look at the graphics in the following exercise to determine the meaning.

EXERCISE 1.23

1. tener frío

2. tener calor

3. tener hambre

4. tener sed

5. tener sueño

6. tener prisa

With this construction, agreement is not necessary. The construction literally means someone *has* hunger, or *has* thirst, as opposed to someone *is* hungry or someone *is* thirsty. Just conjugate *tener*.

EXERCISE 1.24

Determine which physical or mental state best fits the sentences. In some cases, more than one answer may apply.

1. ¡Me tengo que ir ya! ¡Yo _____! Ya son las 8 de la mañana, y mi clase de biología empieza a las 8:15.

2. Bueno, nosotros vamos a comer mucho porque
   _____.

3. Cuando _____ me gusta tomar chocolate caliente.

4. Mis amigos toman cerveza en vez de agua cuando
   _____.

5. Yo siempre _____ cuando estudio para un examen. Como muchas hamburguesas y papas fritas.

6. Maribel se come las uñas (nails) cuando _____.

7. Las personas supersticiosas le _____ a los gatos negros.

8. El director está tan antipático hoy; él _____.

9. Mi madre grita (screams) mucho cuando _____.

DESCRIBING CHANGES IN STATES: *PONERSE*, *HACERSE*, *VOLVERSE*

Ponerse, hacerse, and *volverse* all mean "to become" and are used to describe changes in mental and physical states when followed by adjectives and certain nouns.

Ponerse is used with most adjectives (e.g. *furiosa, nervioso, tímido*).

Hacerse is used with *bueno(a), malo(a), rico(a),* also with religions, *catolico(a)* and professions, *abogado(a).*

Volverse is used with *loco(a).*

> **Se puso muy furioso** cuando leyó tu carta.
> *He became very furious when she read your letter.*

Lisa **se hizo abogada** en tres años.
Lisa became a lawyer in three years.

Rita va a **volverse loca** con todo el trabajo que tiene.
Rita is going to go crazy with all the work she has.

CONOCER VS. SABER

As if trying to figure out the difference between *ser* and *estar* weren't enough, Spanish has yet another pair of verbs that mean the same thing, but are used differently. However, don't worry, these two have (for the most part) regular conjugations, and knowing when to use them is really very straightforward.

The words *conocer* and *saber* both mean "to know." In Spanish, knowing a person or a thing (basically, a noun) is different from knowing a piece of information. Compare these uses of *conocer* and *saber* in these sentences.

¿Sabes cómo se llama el hermano de Rita?
Do you know Rita's brother's name?

Sí, se llama Alejandro. Lo conozco bien.
Yes. His name is Alexander. I know him well.

¿Sabes cuál es la capital de Bolivia?
Do you know the capital of Bolivia?

Sí. Es La Paz. Conozco bien esa cuidad.
Yes. It's La Paz. I know that city well.

When what's known is a person, place, or thing, use *conocer*. It's like the English "acquainted with." When what's known is a fact, use *saber*. The same basic rule holds for questions.

¿Sabes quién es el jefe?
Do you know who the boss is?

Sí, es el Sr. González.
Yes, it is Mr. González.

¿Conoces al jefe personalmente?
Do you know the boss personally?

Sí, conozco al Sr. González personalmente.

Yes, I know Mr. González personally.

Now that you know how they're used, take a look at their conjugations:

conocer — to get to know

Present	Preterite	Future
yo conozco	yo conocí	yo conoceré
tú conoces	tú conocistes	tú conocerás
él/ella/Ud. conoce	él/ella/Ud. conoció	él/ella/Ud. conocerá
nosotros conocemos	nosotros conocimos	nosotros conoceremos
vosotros conocéis	vosotros conocisteis	vosotros conoceréis
ellos/ellas/Uds. conocen	ellos/ellas/Uds. conocieron	ellos/ellas/Uds. conocerán

Conditional	Present Subjunctive	Imperfect Subjunctive
yo conocería	yo conozca	yo conociera
tú conocerías	tú conozcas	tú conocieras
él/ella/Ud. conocería	él/ella/Ud. conozca	él/ella/Ud. conociera
nosotros conoceríamos	nosotros conozcamos	nosotros conociéramos
vosotros conocerías	vosotros cononzcáis	vosotros conociérais
ellos/ellas/Uds. conocerían	ellos/ellas/Uds. conozcan	ellos/ellas/Uds. conocieran

saber — to know

Present	Preterite	Future
yo sé	yo supe	yo sabré
tú sabes	tú supiste	tú sabrás
él/ella/Ud. sabe	él/ella/Ud. supo	él/ella/Ud. sabrá
nosotros sabemos	nosotros supimos	nosotros sabremos
vosotros sabéis	vosotros supisteis	vosotros sabréis
ellos/ellas/Uds. saben	ellos/ellas/Uds. supieron	ellos/ellas/Uds. sabrán

Conditional	Present Subjunctive	Imperfect Subjunctive
yo sabría	yo sepa	yo supiera
tú sabrías	tú sepas	tú supieras
él/ella/Ud. sabría	él/ella/Ud. sepa	él/ella/Ud. supiera
nosotros sabríamos	nosotros sepamos	nosotros supiéramos
vosotros sabríais	vosotros sepáis	vosotros supierais
ellos/ellas/Uds. sabrían	ellos/ellas/Uds. sepan	ellos/ellas/Uds. supieran

MAKING COMPARISONS

COMPARISONS OF INEQUALITY

The comparative of most adjectives, adverbs, and nouns in Spanish is formed by placing *más* (more) or *menos* (less) before the adjective, adverb or noun and then *que*.

> *Más* + adjective /adverb/noun + que
> *Menos* + adjective /adverb/noun + que

California es **más grande que** Maine.

California is larger than Maine.

En mi opinión, la biología es **menos interesante que** la química.

In my opinion, biology is less interesting than chemistry.

¡Tengo pocas ganas de ir a la escuela!

I have little desire to go to school!

¡Yo tengo **menos ganas que** tú!

I have less than you do!

When using an adjective in this construction, the adjective must agree in number and gender with the first noun mentioned.

Los diamantes son **más caros que** las esmeraldas.
Diamonds are more expensive than emeralds.

Las esmeraldas son **menos caras que** los diamantes.
Emeralds are less valuable than diamonds.

COMPARISONS OF EQUALITY

To make comparison of equality with adjectives, adverbs and nouns, use the adverb *tan* or the adjective *tanto, -a, -os, -as* and *como*.

> *Tan* + adjective /adverb/noun + *como*

En mi opinión, la biología es **tan interesante como** la química.

In my opinion, biology is as interesting as chemistry.

Los López tienen **tanto dinero como** los Martín.

The López family has as much money as the Martin family.

Por lo menos no tienes **tantos problemas como** Teresa.

At least you don't have as many problems as Teresa.

En mi casa hay **tantas habitaciones como** en la tuya.

There are as many bedrooms in my house as there are in yours.

THE SUPERLATIVE

The superlative construction is almost identical to the comparative. Simply place the definite article for the person or thing being compared.

Definite article + noun + *más* or *menos* + adjective + *de*

Michael Jordan es el **más alto del** equipo.

Michael Jordan is the tallest one on the team.

Mi madre es la **mejor cocinera del** mundo.

My mother is the best cook in the world.

Mi profesor de español es el **más exigente de** todos.

My Spanish professor is the most demanding of all.

As is the case with the comparative, the adjective must agree in number and gender with the first noun mentioned.

Mi tío es **el hombre más tacaño** del mundo. En cambio, mi tía, es **la mujer más generosa** que conozco.

My uncle is the stingiest man in the world. On the other hand, my aunt is the most generous woman I know.

Use *más de* and *menos de* before a number or quantity.

El *Rolls Royce* del Sr. Ramos tiene un valor de **más de** $50.000.

Mr. Ramos' Rolls Royce has a value of more than $50,000.

Gastamos **menos de** 50.000 pesetas en España.

We spent fewer than 50,000 pesetas in Spain.

Este receta lleva **más de** media libra de pollo.

This recipe calls for more than half a pound of chicken.

Regresamos en **menos de** veinte minutos.

We'll be back in fewer than twenty minutes.

IRREGULAR COMPARATIVE FORMS

The following adjectives and adverbs do not follow the pattern above.

Adjectives	Adverbs	Comparative	Superlative
bueno/a — good	bien — well	mejor — better	el (la) mejor — the best
malo/a — bad	mal — badly	peor — worse	el (la) peor — the worst
grande — big/older		mayor — older	el (la) mayor — the oldest
pequeño/a — small		menor — younger	el (la) menor — the youngest

When talking about size, *grande* and *pequeño* are generally used.

> México es más grande que Bolivia.
> *Mexico is larger than Bolivia.*

> Ecuador es más pequeño que el estado de Texas.
> *Ecuador is smaller than the state of Texas.*

When talking about age, however, the irregular forms are used.

> Mi madre tiene 50 años. Mi padre tiene 55 años. Mi padre es mayor que mi madre. Mi madre es menor que mi padre.
> *My mother is 50 years old. My father is 55 years old. My father is older than my mother. My mother is younger than my father.*

> Pedro Juan es el mayor de los hermanos y María del Pilar es la mayor de las hermanas.
> *Pedro Juan is the oldest of the brothers, and Maria del Pilar is the oldest of the sisters.*

> ¿Los Mets juegan tan bien como los Yankees?
> *Do the Mets play as well as the Yankees?*

> ¡No! ¡Los Yankees juegan mejor que los Mets!

> ¿Marisa cocina tan mal como su madre?
> *Does Marisa cooks as badly as her mother?*

> ¡No, desafortunadamente, Marisa cocina peor que su pobre madre! ¡De hecho, ella es la peor cocinera que conozco!
> *No, unfortunately, Marisa cooks worse than her poor mother does! In fact, she is the worst cook I know!*

EXERCISE 1.25

Fill in the following sentences with the correct form of the adjective, adverb, or noun in parentheses.

1. Michael Jackson es más _____ que Madona. (rico)

2. Los amigos de Pedro son menos _____ que los de María. (extrovertido)

3. Mi mujer es la _____ cocinera del mundo. (bueno)

4. Cindy Crawford es más _____ que Danny DeVito. (alto)

5. Creo que Mario es el _____ de los hermanos. El tiene 96 años. (viejo)

OBJECTS AND OBJECT PRONOUNS

The noun directly affected by the action of the verb is the direct object.

> Los británicos extrañan a la Princesa Diana.
>
> *The English miss Princess Diana.*

The Verb: miss

Who? What? Princess Diana.

Princess Diana is the direct object.

> Los Beatles cantaron "Yesterday."
>
> *The Beatles sang "Yesterday."*

Who? What? "Yesterday"

"Yesterday" is the direct object.

PERSONAL A

When the direct object is a person, *a* must precede it. This is called the *personal a*.

Example:

> No conozco a la Reina Sofía de España, pero si conozco Madrid, la capital española.
>
> *I don't know the Queen Sofia of Spain, but I am familiar with Madrid, the Spanish capital.*

La Reina is a person, thus *a la Reina*, while *Madrid* is a place, and so the personal *a* is *not* included.

EXERCISE 1.26

Underline the direct object in the following sentences.

1. Los Beatles tienen canciones famosas.

2. Los norteamericanos compran muchos discos ingleses.

3. Los españoles estudian inglés en sus universidades.

4. La iglesia ayuda mucho a los pobres.

INDIRECT OBJECT

The indirect object is the noun or pronoun that answers the question to whom? or for whom? After determining the verb, ask to whom? or for whom? Let's examine the sentences below. Follow the series of questions to determine the direct and indirect objects of a sentence.

Example:

> Gerald Ford le otorgó un perdón a Nixon
> *Gerald Ford granted Nixon a pardon.*

What is the verb? *granted*

> Who or what did Ford grant? *a pardon*
> *Pardon* is the direct object.

To whom or for whom did Ford grant the pardon? *Nixon*

> *Nixon* is the indirect object.

Example:

> José le hizo un favor a mi amigo.
> *José did my friend a favor.*

What is the verb? *hizo* (preterit of **hacer**—to do)
Who or what did *José* do? *un favor.*

> *Favor* is the direct object.

To whom or for whom did *José* do *un favor? mi amigo.*

> *Mi amigo* is the indirect object.

EXERCISE 1.27

Match the following sentences to their translation:

1.	El policía los sacó del bar a la fuerza.	A	My parents love me very much.
2.	José la invito a una cena elegante.	B	José and María took us to the party last night.
3.	Mis padres me quieren mucho.	C	The police took them out of the bar forcefully.
4.	José y María nos llevaron a la fiesta anoche.	D	I took him to the doctor last night.
5.	Tú has cambiado. Ya no te conozco.	E	You've changed. I don't know you anymore.
6.	Yo lo llevé al médico anoche.	F	José treated her to an elegant dinner.

DIRECT OBJECT PRONOUNS

Direct object pronouns take the place of the direct object in a sentence.

> Los británicos extrañan a **la** Princesa Diana. Los británicos **la** extrañan.

> The British miss Princess Diana. The British miss **her**.

Choosing the correct pronouns depends on the person, number, and gender of the direct object. In the sentence above, *Princesa Diana* is singular, feminine, and in the third person (she is being spoken about), so the corresponding direct object pronoun, *la*, is used.

PLACEMENT OF OBJECT PRONOUNS

The direct object pronouns come before the conjugated verb. In all the sentences above, the direct object pronoun immediately precedes the verb.

> Los británicos la extrañan.

> ¿Las hamburguesas? Yo no **las** como.

> El me conoce bien.

Yo te quiero mucho.

Nosotros lo vimos anoche en la fiesta.

¡Yo os ayudé demasiado!

Ella los llevó al aeropuerto esta mañana.

The direct object pronouns are	The indirect object pronouns are
me — me	me — to me
te — you	te — to you
lo — him	le — to him/to her/ to you (formal)
la — her	nos — to us
nos — we	os — to you (plural)
os — you (plural)	les — to them/to you (plural)
los — they (masculine)	
las — they (feminine)	

INDIRECT OBJECT PRONOUNS

These pronouns replace the indirect object. Like the direct object pronouns, they come *before* the conjugated verb.

Gerald Ford le otorgó un perdón a Nixon.

Le refers to Nixon in this case.

The indirect object pronoun is obligatory. In the following sentence, the *le* must be included.

Gerald Ford le otorgó un perdón.

It would be grammatically incorrect to write *Gerald Ford otorgó perdón a Nixon*. To an English speaker, however, that sounds fine because in English we would say, "Gerald Ford granted Nixon a pardon."

In Spanish, *a* + the indirect object is optional. It does, however, clarify a great deal. In this sentence, *"Gerald Ford le otorgó perdón a Nixon,"* a Nixon tells us that *le* refers to *Nixon*.

Look at this example:

La profesora le explica el concepto.

The profesor explains the concept.

The sentence is grammatically correct. The question is, To whom does she explain the concept. Does *le* refer to him, to her, to you formal?

La profesora le explica el concepto a Rita.

The prepositional phrase *a Rita* gives far more information. We know that Rita is the indirect object. For English speakers, this seems redundant, and in fact it is. You are referring to the same indirect object twice, once in the form of a pronoun and then again in the form of a noun. But this is grammatically correct in Spanish.

2

Talking About The Past

There are several ways to express the past tense in Spanish. You can talk about what just happened, what happened in the past, or what used to happen.

TALKING ABOUT WHAT JUST HAPPENED

A form of *acabar* + *de* + an infinitive is used to talk about something that just happened. Keep in mind, however, that the passage of time is relative. The following are all correct uses of the structure.

> Acabo de hablar con Jorge por teléfono hace dos minutos.
>
> *I just spoke to George on the phone two minutes ago.*

> Acabamos de regresar del viaje. Llegamos hace una semana.
>
> *We just got back from the trip. We arrived a week ago.*

Relative to the speaker's point of view, both are in the immediate past. The second sentence could be in the preterite, but using this structure emphasizes the speaker's perception that their return was relatively recent.

Note: *Acabar* can be in any tense. For example, you could say, "*Acabábamos de entrar a la casa cuando sonó el teléfono.*" "We had just walked into the house when the phone rang." For our purposes, however, let's just look at the present indicative.

FORMATION

To form the construction, simply conjugate the verb *acabar*, then add *de* and an infivitive. *Acabamos de graduarnos de la universidad.* (We just graduated from college.) *Nosotros* is the subject, so we need *acabamos*. If *yo* were the subject, it would read, *Acabo de graduarme de la universidad.*

acabar—to finish	
Singular	**Plural**
yo acabo	nosotros acabamos
tú acabas	vosotros acabáis
él/ella/Ud. acaba	ellos/ellas/Uds. acaban

EXERCISE 2.1

Give the correct form of the verb *acabar* in each of the following sentences.

1. Mis abuelos _____ de mudarse a la Florida.

2. Ricky Martin _____ de ganar un premio Grammy.

3. Yo _____ de depositar mi cheque en el banco.

4. Los estudiantes _____ de salir de clase.

5. Mi mujer y yo _____ de comprarnos una casa.

TALKING ABOUT WHAT HAPPENED

To talk about events that occurred at a specific point in time in the past, use the preterite tense.

Examples:

> Yo fui a Argentina en 1987.
> *I went to Argentina in 1987.*

Los alemanes ocuparon París durante la segunda guerra mundial.

The Germans occupied Paris during World War II.

Recibimos el telegrama esta mañana.

We received the telegram this morning.

FORMATION

To form the preterite, of regular verbs, simply:

1. Drop the *-ar*, *-er*, or *-ir* ending of the infinitive.

2. Add the following endings.

Preterite

Regular endings	-AR	-ER	-IR
yo	-é	-í	-í
tú	-aste	-iste	-iste
él/ella/Ud.	-ó	-ió	-ió
nosostros	-amos	-imos	-imos
vosotros	-asteis	-isteis	-isteis
ellos/ellas/Uds.	-aron	-ieron	-ieron

EXERCISE 2.2

Give the correct form of the verb in parentheses. All the verbs are regular in the preterite.

1. Yo _____ (hablar) con mi novia anoche.

2. Muchos chinos _____ (inmigrar) a Cuba durante el siglo XIX.

3. Mis amigos _____ (comer) en un restaurante chileno.

4. José no _____ (beber) anoche en la fiesta.

5. La iglesia católica _____ (participar) en el desfile.

EXERCISE 2.3

Answer the following yes or no questions about your day yesterday. Answer in a full sentence.

1. ¿Saliste (tú) con tus amigos ayer?

2. ¿Estudiaste (tú) en la biblioteca?

3. ¿Trabajaste (tú) más de ocho horas?

4. ¿Comiste (tú) algún dulce ayer?

5. ¿Llamaste a (tu) mejor amigo?

IRREGULAR VERBS IN THE PRETERITE

The following verbs are irregular in the preterite. Some of the irregular preterite verbs have the same endings. Just add the following ending to the indicated root.

(yo)	(tu)	él/ella/Ud.	nos.	vos.	ellos/ellas/Uds.
-e	-iste	-o	-imos	-isteís	-ieron

andar: anduv-

estar: estuv-

hacer: hic/hiz-

poder: pud-

poner: pus-

querer: quis-

saber: sup-

venir: vin-

Example:

Estar—to be

	Singular	Plural
	yo estuve	nosotros estuvimos
	tú estuviste	vosotros/estuvisteis
	él-/ella/Ud./estuvo	ellos/ellas/Uds./estivieron

The following irregular verbs have stems that end in *j*.

The endings are: *-e, -iste, -o, -imos, -isteis, -eron*

  conducir: conduj-

  decir: dij-

  traducir: traduj-

  traer: traj-

EXERCISE 2.4

The following sentences are in the preterite. Give the appropriate form of the verb in parentheses.

1. Los trovadores _____ por el barrio cantando anoche. (andar)

2. ¿_____ los romanos en España? (estar)

3. Cuando el pinchadiscos _____ nuestra canción preferida nos pusimos a bailar. (poner).

4. Mi hermano _____ un coche de cambios cuando estuvimos en Málaga de vacaciones. (conducir)

5. Yo le _____ a la profesora que estabas enferma. (decir)

SER AND IR

Ser (to be) and *ir* (to go) are identical in the preterite. Only the context differentiates them.

  Examples:

  ¿Tu hermano fue a Madrid el año pasado?

  Your brother went to Madrid last year?

  ¿Quién fue el autor de ese libro?

  Who was the author of that book?

Ser/ir — to be/to go

	Singular	Plural
	yo fui	nosostros fuimos
	tú fuiste	vosotros fuisteis
	él/ella/Ud. fue	ellos/ellas/Uds. fueron

EXERCISE 2.5

Determine which verb (*ser* or *ir*) is being used in the following sentences. Use the context to help you.

1. Colombia *fue* el primer país que se independizó de España. _____

2. Nosotros *fuimos* muy serviciales con Adal. No entiendo su actitud. _____

3. Mis padres no *fueron* a México conmigo. _____

4. Cuando *fuimos* al supermercado, José nos esperó en el carro. _____

5. Marco Antonio *fue* un emperador romano. _____

Verbs ending in *-car*, *-gar*, and *-zar* in the infinitive form have the following ending changes before the *é* in the *yo* form.

Examples:

sacar (to take out) becomes *yo saqué*

rogar (to beg) becomes *rogué*

calzar (to wear, e.g. shoes) becomes *calcé*

These are the changes:

   c   becomes *qu*

   g   becomes *gu*

   z   becomes *c*

Some verbs that end in -car

   abanicar—to fan

   abarcar—to cover

   acercarse—to approach

   brincar—to jump

   buscar—to look for

   calificar—to grade

   chocar—to crash

   colocar—to place

   complicar—to complicate

comunicar—to communicate

criticar—to criticize

dedicar—to dedicate

educar—to educate

equivocarse—to make a mistake

explicar—to explain

identificar—to identify

marcar—to mark

pescar—to fish

picar—to bite, to sting

practicar—to practice

secar—to dry

Some verbs that end in -gar

abrigar—to cherish (an idea)

agregar—to add

ahogarse—to drown

apagar—to turn off

cargar—to carry, load

castigar—to punish

colgar—to hang

despegar—to take off

encargar—to order (merchandise)

entregar—to deliver

halagar—to flatter

juzgar—to judge

ligar—to bind

llegar—to arrive

negar—to deny

pagar—to pay

rasgar—to tear

regar—to water (plants)

rogar—to beg

Some verbs that end in -zar

abrazar—to hug

alcanzar—to reach

almorzar—to have lunch

aterrizar—to land

autorizar—to authorize

bautizar—to baptize

bostezar—to yawn

calzar—to wear

colonizar—to colonize

comenzar—to begin

cruzar—to cross

danzar—to dance

esforzar—to strain

garantizar—to guarantee

gozar (de)—to enjoy

lanzar—to throw

organizar—to organize

realizar—to execute

rezar—to pray

ridiculizar—to ridicule

sollozar—to sob

tranquilizar(se)—to calm down

tropezar—to trip

utilizar—to use

EXERCISE 2.6

Give the correct preterite form of the verb in parenthesis.

1. Cuando yo _____ (empezar) mi viaje, tenía mucho miedo.

2. Los estudiantes _____ (utilizar) las computadoras en la biblioteca.

3. Yo _____ (encargarse) del asunto.

4. Cuando llegamos a Buenos Aires, yo _____ (cargar) todo el equipaje.

5. Yo _____ (sacar) estas fotos para ti.

In the preterite, *dar* (to give) and *ver* (to see) take the endings for *-er* and *-ir* verbs, respectively. Note that there is no accent mark in the *yo* and *él* forms of these verbs.

dar — to give

Singular	Plural
yo di	nosotros dimos
tú diste	vosotros disteis
él/ella/Ud. dio	ellos/ellas/Uds. dieron

ver — to see

Singular	Plural
yo vi	nosotros vimos
tú viste	vosotros visteis
él/ella/Ud. vio	ellos/ellas/Uds. vieron

Oír (to hear), *caer* (to fall), and verbs ending in *-eer* and *-uir* change in the *él* and *ellos* form. The *i* becomes *y* to break up the stringing together of three vowels.

oír — to hear

	Singular	Plural
	yo oí	nosotros oímos
	tú oíste	vosotros oísteis
	él/ella/Ud. oyó	ellos/ellas/Uds. oyeron

caer — to fall

	Singular	Plural
	yo caí	nosotros caímos
	tú caíste	vosotros caísteis
	él/ella/Ud. cayo	ellos/ellas/Uds. cayeron

leer — to read

	Singular	Plural
	yo leí	nosotros leímos
	tú leíste	vosotros leísteis
	él/ella/Ud. leyó	ellos/ellas/Uds. leyeron

STEM-CHANGING VERBS

All stem-changing -ar verbs are regular in the preterite. The stem-changing verbs in the present do NOT have stem changes in the preterite. For example, the verb *pensar* is *yo pienso* in the present, but *yo pensé* in the preterite.

Some stem-changing verbs in the present to watch out for:

pensar [ie]—to think

contar [ue]—to count

jugar [ue]—to play

perder [ie]—to lose

volver [ue]—to return

EXERCISE 2.7

Write the correct preterite form of the verb in parentheses.

1. José Martí, el escritor cubano _____ que Cuba tenía que luchar en contra del dominio de España. (pensar)

2. Antonio y Rita _____ béisbol en el parque el domingo pasado. (jugar)

3. _____ los libros de Dickens cuando éramos niños. (leer)

4. Yo le _____ a Elena toda la información que quería. (dar)

5. ¿_____Uds. los disparos anoche? (oír)

The -ir verbs that have a stem change in the present have the following stem changes only in the él and ellos form in the preterite.

sentir — to feel

e – i	Singular	Plural
	yo sentí	nosotros sentimos
	tú sintiste	vosotros sentisteis
	él/ella/Ud. sintió	ellos/ellas/Uds. sintieron

dormir — to sleep

o – u	Singular	Plural
	yo dormí	nosotros dormimos
	tú durmiste	vosotros dormisteis
	él/ella/Ud. durmió	ellos/ellas/Uds. durmieron

Here are some additional -ir stem-changing verbs that follow this pattern.

advertir—to warn

divertir—to amuse

divertirse—to amuse oneself

mentir—to lie

pedir—to ask for

preferir—to prefer

repetir—to repeat

seguir—to follow

sentirse—to feel

servir—to serve

sonreir—to smile

EXERCISE 2.8

Give the correct form of the indicated verb.

1. El delincuente le _____ (mentir) al juez.

2. Los amigos de José _____ (preferir) salir a bailar anoche.

3. Yo le _____ (servir) un arroz con pollo.

4. Nosotros _____ (divertirse) mucho en el parque de diversiones.

5. Las autoridades le _____ (advertir) que era peligroso volar esa avioneta.

HAY AND HACER

The preterite of *hay* is *hubo.*

> Hubo un accidente terrible en la carretera.
> *There was a terrible accident on the highway.*

> Hubo miles de personas en el concierto.
> *There were thousands of people at the concert.*

Expressing ago: *hacer + time*

> *Hace* followed by a period of time is equivalent to *ago* in English.

> Hace una hora—*an hour ago*

> Hace tres minutos—*three minutes ago*

> Hace menos de un semana—*less than a week ago*

> Hace años—*years ago*

To ask how long ago did, you can either ask:

¿Cuánto (tiempo) hace que + verb in the preterite

or

¿Hace cuánto (tiempo) que + verb in the preterite

¿Cuánto (tiempo) hace que Uds. se casaron?
How long ago did you get married?

Hace dos años y medio.
Two and a half years ago.

TALKING ABOUT WHAT *USED TO* HAPPEN

The imperfect is yet another past tense used to describe actions that occurred on an ongoing basis in the past and exhibited no definitive end at that time. The preterite tense, on the other hand, describes "one-time" actions that began and ended at the moment in the past being discussed. Look at the two together and the difference between them will become clearer.

Mis amigos y yo bailamos en la fiesta de anoche hasta las dos de la mañana.
My friends and I danced at the party last night until two in the morning.

We know that the dancing ended because they did it until a specific time in the past. Therefore, the preterite makes sense here.

Hablábamos mientras bailábamos.
We talked while we danced.

The talking was happening during the dancing. The actions in this sentence have no specific beginning or ending time. The imperfect is used in this case.

Perfect—in grammatical terms—means complete and imperfect means incomplete. That's why the imperfect is used to express actions that do not have a definitive beginning or end in the past.

The imperfect is also used to describe conditions or circumstances in the past, since these are obviously ongoing occurrences.

Hacía buen tiempo y estábamos de buen humor.
The weather was good and we were in a good mood.

Cuando era estudiante universitario, me encantaban mis clases de literatura.
When I was a college student, I used to love my literature classes.

In the first example, the weather neither started nor ended. The weather was in progress and so was our good mood. That is why the imperfect is appropriate there.

In the second example, the actions described also occurred on an ongoing basis in the past and exhibited no definitive end at that time. Therefore the imperfect is appropriate there.

La primera vez que fui a Nueva York tenía quince años.
I was fifteen the first time I went to New York.

Fui is in the preterite tense. It refers to a specific event. We can determine exactly when it happened.

Tenía, on the other hand, is in the imperfect because it refers to the speaker's age at the time of the trip; this was an existing condition at the time.

FORMATION

The good news is that forming the imperfect is not difficult and there are only three irregular verbs—that's rare!

The Imperfect

	hablar	comer/vivir
yo	-aba	-ía
tú	-abas	-ías
él/ella/Ud.	-aba	-ía
nosostros	-ábamos	-íamos
vosotros	-abais	-íais
ellos/ellas/Uds.	-aban	-ían

	ir	**ser**	**ver**
yo	iba	era	veía
tú	ibas	eras	veías
él/ella/Ud.	iba	era	veía
nosotros	íbamos	éramos	veíamos
vosotros	ibais	erais	veíais
elos/ellas/Uds.	iban	eran	veían

EXERCISE 2.9

María asks her grandmother about her childhood in rural Mexico. Write out their conversation. Change the infinitive verbs to the imperfect.

1. Abuela, ¿cuál/ser/su juego preferido de niña?

2. yo/jugar/a la bebeleche con mis hermanas.

3. ¿Tener/Ud./tareas en la casa?

4. Sí, María. Yo/ayudar/a mi madre en la cocina. Yo/preparar/ la cena para todo el mundo cuando ella/tener/que trabajar fuera de la casa.

5. La vida en el campo/ser/dura, pero divertida también.

PRETERITE VS. IMPERFECT

PRETERITE TENSE

Use the preterite when referring to:

1. a specific action that happened a specific number of times in the past.

   Lo llamé tres veces anoche.

   I called him three times last night.

2. actions that occurred at a specific time.

   Hablamos con María desde las 5 hasta las 7.

   We spoke to María from 5 to 7.

3. the main action

Les expliqué el concepto.

I explained the idea to them.

IMPERFECT TENSE

Use the imperfect when referring to:

1. a repeated habitual action that took place an unspecified number of times.

Yo siempre lo llamaba.

I always called him.

2. actions that were happening or going on for an unspecified period of time.

Yo estudiaba mientras mi madre preparaba la cena.

I studied while my mother prepared dinner.

3. the background or circumstances of the main actions, for example:

4. time and weather

Eran las nueve y ya llovía cuando al avión aterrizó.

It was nine and it was already raining when the plane landed.

5. age; physical appearance

Cuando tenía 18 años, ella era muy guapa.

When she was 18, she was very pretty.

6. feelings, beliefs/emotional states

Pensaba que estaba desilusionada conmigo. Por eso me sentía tan mal.

I thought you were disappointed in me. That's why I felt so bad.

7. external circumstances and actions in progress.

Estábamos bailando cuando llegó la policía.

We were dancing when the police arrived.

EXERCISE 2.10

Determine whether the given verb should be in the preterite or in the imperfect.

1. Cuando yo tenía 10 años, _____ (ir) todos los días a casa de mi tía Cuca.

2. El día que la española fue a casa, le _____ (dar) cien dólares.

3. Mis padres _____ (llegar) anoche a las 10.

4. Mis primos _____ (estudiar) en México desde junio a diciembre.

5. Ellos _____ (estar) estudiando cuando los llamé.

USING THE PRETERITE AND THE IMPERFECT IN THE SAME SENTENCE

Conocí a María cuando era estudiante universitario.
I met María when I was a college student.

Pensé en mis padres mientras lavaba los platos.
I thought about my parents while I was washing the dishes.

Cuando llegué, José hablaba por teléfono.
When I arrived, José was talking on the phone.

Vi a una mujer que tocaba la guitarra en el metro.
I saw a woman who was playing the guitar in the subway.

You can use the imperfect and the preterite in the same sentence. Be aware of the relationship of the actions.

Action at a specific time	Action in progress
Cuando te vi	*yo esperaba el autobús*
Encontramos un gato	*que necesitaba mucho cariño*

In the sentence *Cuando te vi yo esperaba el autobús*, the waiting was in progress when I saw you. The same applies to the second sentence: *Encontramos un gato que necesitaba mucho cariño, necesitaba* refers to an existing condition. The cat was essentially in the middle of needing a lot of affection when *we* found it. The act of finding, if you will, took place at a specific moment, thus the preterite.

EXERCISE 2.11

Change the following present tense passage to the past. Some verbs need to be in the preterite while others in the imperfect.

Es el domingo por la noche. Son las tres de la mañana. Hace mucho calor en la casa de la Sra. Miranda. Todas las ventanas están abiertas y la Sra. Miranda duerme profundamente en su cuarto. A las tres en punto, un joven pasa por el frente de la casa. Tiene 21 años. Es alto, fuerte y lleva bigotes. El entra por la ventana de la sala y se sienta en el sofá. Admira las pinturas en la pared y los muebles elegantes. Después de unos minutos va a la cocina, abre el refrigerador y ve que hay mucha comida. Se prepara un sándwich de pollo y se sirve un vaso de vino tinto. Se sienta a la mesa del comedor, come y bebe tranquilamente. Mientras come, piensa que la señora Miranda es muy buena cocinera. Se come todo el sándwich y se toma la botella entera de vino. Se emborracha tanto que cae al piso y el ruido despierta a la Sra. Miranda. Asustada, baja las escaleras con una pistola en las manos y descubre un hombre en la cocina. Al acercarse y mirarle la cara, se da cuenta de que es José, su jardinero que duerme profundamente en el piso. De repente siente una brisa fuerte y se da cuenta de que están abiertas las ventanas. Va a cerrarlas, sonríe y regresa a su cama.

THE IMPERFECT PROGRESSIVE

To talk about what was happening in the past, use the imperfect progressive.

Yo me estaba duchando cuando me llamaste.

I was taking a shower when you called.

El profesor estaba revisando los exámenes cuando llamaron a la puerta.

The professor was correcting the exams when they knocked at the door.

To form the imperfect progressive, use the imperfect of *estar* + the present participle.

You only need to conjugate *estar*. There is only one form of the present participle for each verb. Look at the following chart:

Estar	Present Participle
Yo estaba	llamando
tú estabas	llamando
él, ella, Ud. estaba	llamando
nosotros estábamos	llamando
vosotros estabais	llamando
ellos, ellas, Uds. estaban	llamando

EXERCISE 2.12

Give the imperfect progressive of each of the verbs in parentheses.

1. Cuando estabámos en la escuela primaria, siempre
   _____ (jugar) en el patio a la hora del recreo.

2. La madre de Josefina _____ (llorar) cuando la vi.

3. Estabámos tan contentos de que finalmente _____
   _____ (tomar) vacaciones.

4. ¿Qué _____ (hacer) Pedro y Carlos cuando los
   fuiste a ver anoche?

5. Ellos les _____ (preparar) una cena ligera a
   Susana y a Margarita.

EXPRESSIONS OF TIME

ayer—yesterday

anteayer—the day before yesterday

un día—one day

el día anterior—the day before

el otro día—the other day

una vez—once

alguna vez—some time

dos veces—twice

por primera vez—for the first time

de repente—suddenly

de pronto—suddenly

por fin—finally

finalmente—finally

antes—before

en el pasado—in the past

a veces—sometimes

de vez en cuando—once in a while

siempre—always

a menudo—often

raramente—rarely

rara vez—rare occasion

por lo general—in general

generalmente—generally

usualmente—usually

THE PRESENT PERFECT

The present perfect is used to refer to an action that began in the past and is continuing into the present (and possibly beyond). It is also used to describe actions that were completed very close to the present. Compare these sentences.

1. Ayer hablé con mis amigos.
   Yesterday I spoke to my friends.
   Decidiste no ir al cine.
   You decided not to go the movies.

2. He hablado mucho con mis amigos recientemente.
   I have spoken a lot to my friends lately.
   Has decidido hacerte abogado.
   You have decided (recently) to become a lawyer.

The first examples are just the plain past tense: you started and finished talking with your friends yesterday and you completed the process of deciding not to go to the movies. In the second examples, the use of the present perfect tense moves the action to the very recent past, instead of leaving it in the distant past. The present perfect, then, is essentially a more precise verb form of the past, used when the speaker wants to indicate that an action happened very recently in the past.

The present perfect is a compound tense, meaning that it is formed by combining two verbs, the auxiliary or helping verb *haber* and the past participle of the main verb. Remember: perfect means total, complete.

FORMATION

Present of haber

he

has

ha

hemos

habéis

han

To form the past participle of most verbs, drop the last two letters of the infinitive form and add *-ado* (for *-ar* verbs) and *-ido* (for *-er* and *-ir* verbs).

Past Participle

-ar	ado
hablar	hablado
-er	**ido**
comer	comido
-ir	**ido**
vivir	vivido

There are some irregular past participles

abrir—to open
abierto

cubrir—to cover
cubierto

decir—to say
  dicho

escribir—to write
  escrito

hacer—to do
  hecho

imprimir—to print
  impreso

morir—to die
  muerto

poner—to put
  puesto

romper—to break
  roto

ver—to see
  visto

volver—to return
  vuelto

EXERCISE 2.13

Give the present perfect of the verbs in parentheses.

1. Más mujeres _____ (lograr) un alto grado de indepencia.

2. Una amiga de María _____ (tener) que dejar sus estudios porque no le renovaron la beca.

3. La jueza y el abogado _____ (llegar) a un acuerdo.

4. Yo _____ (cambiar) de profesión por motivos económicos.

5. Nosotros _____ (decidir) divorciarnos.

EXERCISE 2.14

Have you ever done any of the following? Create the question, then answer it.

Example: Volaré en el Concorde.

¿Ha volado en el Concorde?

Si, he volado en el Concorde tres veces.

1. manejar un Mercedes Benz

2. bailar el cha-cha-chá

3. asistir a clases de matemáticas

4. hacer una fiesta en tu casa

5. estar en Buenos Aires

THE PAST PERFECT

The preterite describes actions that were completed in the past. To describe actions that were completed before a specific point in the past, Spanish speakers use the past perfect tense. Some refer to it as the "the past of the past."

Cuando me llamaste por teléfono, ya me había bañado.
When you called me on the phone, I had already taken a bath.

José había terminado sus estudios universitarios antes de casarse.
José had finished college before he got married.

The past perfect is also used in indirect speech (speech that repeats or reports but does not quote someone's words) when the declarative verb is in the preterite and reference is made to a previous action.

El presentador dijo que el Presidente había firmado el tratado.
The newscaster said the president had signed the treaty.

Time line marking the present, the past, and the past perfect for milestones in Enrique's life.

22 years old	25 years old	30 years old
había terminado sus estudios	se casó con María	tiene dos niños
past perfect	**past**	**present**

Enrique finished college when he was 22. He got married at 25. At 30 years of age, he has two children.

FORMATION

The past perfect is formed as follows:

Imperfect of haber + past participle

Imperfect of *haber*

haber — to have

Singular	Plural
yo había	nosotros habíamos
tú habías	vosotros habíais
él/ella/Ud. había	ellos/ellas/Uds. habían

The past participles are presented above. See Present perfect.

EXERCISE 2.15

Jose's family immigrated to the United States from Cuba. Tell what they had or had not done before coming.

1. Mi madre/nunca/hablar/inglés.

2. Mi padre/ya/estudiar/medicina.

3. Nosotros/nunca/ver/la nieve.

4. Mis tías/nunca/manejar/un auto.

5. Yo/nunca/ver/Disneyland.

EXERCISE 2.16

Using the pairs of sentences below, tell what had already happened (the second sentence) by the time the first one took place. The first sentence is in the present indicative. Change it to the preterite. The second sentence is in the preterite. Change it to the past perfect.

Example:

Yo llego al aeropuerto. El vuelo despegó.

Cuando llegué al aeropuerto, el vuelo ya había despegado.

1. Decides ir al cine. La película empezó.

   Cuando_____

2. Enciendes el televisor. Tu programa preferido se terminó.

   Cuando_____

3. Vas a la tienda para comprar un nuevo programa para la computadora. Se agotó.

   Cuando_____

4. Buscas a un amigo en un "Chat Room." Se desconectó de la Red.

   Cuando_____

5. Sacas la tarjeta de crédito para pagar. Pasó su fecha de expiración.

   Cuando_____

DESCRIBING ACTIONS: *ADVERBS*

Adverbs describe actions, or verbs. They tell us when, where, how, and why.

Adverbs are easy to create in Spanish. In most cases, adverbs are formed by simply adding -*mente* to the feminine or neuter form of an adjective. The adverb maintains any written accent from the adjective form.

sincera (*sincere*) is the adjective; **sinceramente** (*sincerely*) is the adverb.

feliz (*happy*) becomes **felizmente** (*happily*)

actual (*present*) becomes **actualmente** (*presently*)

rápido (*fast*) becomes **rápidamente** (*fast*).

cómodo (*comfortable*) becomes **cómodamente** (*comfortably*)

Antonio, ¿preparas el desayuno **frecuentemente**?
Anthony, do you prepare breakfast often?

No, sólo los domingos.
No, only on Sundays.

¿Qué pasó en el juicio ayer?
What happened during the trial yesterday?

El delincuente se confesó **públicamente**.
The criminal confessed publicly.

If two adverbs are used back to back, both are in their feminine or neuter form and only the second one takes the *-mente* suffix.

Necesito una computadora que funcione **rápida** y **silenciosamente**.
I need a computer that works quickly and silently.

Adverbs of Place

To tell *where* an action happened, use the adverbs of place.

here	there	over there
aquí	ahí	allí
acá	allí	allá

Other adverbs of place

arriba — *up, upstairs*	abajo — *down, downstairs*
adentro — *in, inside*	afuera — *out, outside*
enfrente — *in front, across, opposite*	atrás — *back, in back*

3

You Want Me To Do What?

So far we have looked at verbal constructions that express facts and/or ask questions. Now let's move into the area of Spanish grammar that makes even the strictest grammarians a little loco: the subjunctive.

WHAT IS THE SUBJUNCTIVE?

In order to talk about the subjunctive, we first must differentiate tense from mood.

Tense refers to when an action occurs. An action can occur in the present, preterit, imperfect, or the future.

Mood indicates the attitude the speaker has toward an action. The moods are the *indicative, imperative,* and *subjunctive.*

The indicative mood is objective. It is used to discuss a fact or facts, and is considered to be definite or certain.

The imperative mood is used to give commands, which may be formal or informal.

The subjunctive mood is subjective. It is used to express feelings, emotions, and judgments in connection to an action. It is also used to express what *may* be or what *might* be.

Compare these sentences:

Indicative	Subjunctive	Imperative
I *feel* terrible.	I wish I *felt* better.	*Feel* better.
You *are* free.	It is fair that all people *be* free.	*Be* free.
José *speaks* Spanish in class.	The teacher recommends José *speak* only English in class.	*Speak* English.

The sentences in the indicative column simply state facts, while those in the subjunctive column express desire, opinion. The Imperative ones state orders.

The key concept to keep in mind with the subjunctive tense is influence. When we say that we wish, prefer, desire, ask, or demand someone to do something, or if we say that it is ridiculous, amazing, or terrific that something has happened, we are either directly influencing the action, or at least putting the influence of our opinion over the action. If we are happy, sad, scared, or excited that something has happened, it is the event itself that is influencing us and our emotions.

Look at these factual statements.

José es tu jefe.
José is your boss.

¿Fue José mi jefe?
Was José your boss?

José será tu próximo jefe.
José will be your next boss.

The first sentence states the simple fact that is in the present, thus the present indicative. The second sentence asks a question about a fact in the past, thus it is in the preterit. The last sentence states something so likely to happen, we can treat it like a fact. All three are in the indicative mood. But when we talk about feelings, attitudes, and emotions, we can not talk about things as if they were facts.

DEPENDENT AND INDEPENDENT CLAUSES

The subjunctive means "subordinate." That should help you remember that the subjunctive is used in the dependent (or *subordinate*) clause. Look at the following examples. The verb of the independent clause is in the indicative while the dependent (or *subordinate)* clause is in the subjunctive.

Independent Clause	Dependent Clause
Les recomiendo	que vayan a ver "Star Wars".
I suggest	(that) you go see Star Wars.
(Nosotros) esperamos	que (tú) estés bien.
We hope	(that) you are well.
(Yo) lamento	que (tú) tengas que pasar por esto.
I'm sorry	(that) you have to go through this.

Examples:

El médico insiste en que yo haga más ejercicio.
The doctor insists that I do more exercise.

El psicólogo me sugiere que yo sea menos paranoico.
The psychologist suggests I be less paraonoid.

Mi novia quiere que yo le dé un anillo de compromiso.
My girfriend wants me to give her an engagement ring.

When there are at least two different subjects in a sentence, the subjunctive is used. If there is only one subject in a sentence, the indicative tense is used rather than the subjunctive.

One Subject	Two Different Subjects
Yo siento tener que hacer esto.	Yo siento que José tenga que hacer esto.
I am sorry I have to do this.	I am sorry that José has to do this.
Nosotros queremos hablar con el gerente.	Nosotros queremos que la gerencia hable con nosotros.
We want to talk to the manager.	We want the management to talk to us.

FORMATION OF THE SUBJUNCTIVE

The root for the subjunctive is based on the *yo* form of the present indicative.

Follow these easy steps below and you'll get it right every time. Let's work with *hablar*.

1. What is your verb? *hablar*

2. What is the *yo* form in the present indicative? *hablo*

3. Drop the *-o* ending. *habl-* is your root to form the present subjunctive.

4. Add the following endings for *-ar* verbs.

-e; -es; -e; -emos; -éis; -en

So, the conjugations are:

hablar—to talk

Singular	Plural
yo hable	nosotros hablemos
tú hables	vosotros habléis
él/ella/Ud. hable	ellos/ellas/Uds. hablen

Follow the same steps (1–3) for *-er* and *-ir* verbs, but add the following endings.

-a; -as; -a; -amos; -áis; -an

Let's try *comer* this time.

comer—to eat

Singular	Plural
yo coma	nosotros comamos
tú comas	vosotros comáis
él/ella/Ud. coma	ellos/ellas/Uds. coman

Finally, let's take a look at *vivir*.

vivir — to live

Singular	Plural
yo viva	nosotros vivamos
tú vivas	vosotros viváis
él/ella/Ud. viva	ellos/ellas/uds. vivan

EXERCISE 3.1

Give the present subjunctive of the regular verbs in the following sentences.

1. Sus padres desean que ellos _____ (vivir) en su casa.

2. Es aconsejable que Uds. _____ (comer) antes de salir.

3. Su profesora quiere que Ud. _____ (bailar) con nosotras.

4. Es recomendable que sus estudiantes _____ (hablar) sólo español en clase

5. El agente de viajes nos recomienda que nosotros _____ (viajar) antes del 25 de diciembre.

Certain verbs have an irregular *yo* form in the present indicative. Here are their stems.

	Present Indicative	Present Subjunctive
venir	yo vengo	que yo venga
conducir	yo conduzco	que yo conduzca
construir	yo construyo	que yo construya
recoger	yo recojo	que yo recoja
poner	yo pongo	que yo ponga
oír	yo oigo	que yo oiga
decir	yo digo	que yo diga
mantener	yo mantengo	que yo mantenga
obtener	yo obtengo	que yo obtenga

Note: The endings are the same as the regular verbs in the present subjunctive. Only the root is different.

EXERCISE 3.2

Give the present subjunctive of the irregular verbs in the following sentences.

1. Necesito que ellos _____ (poner) las cosas en su lugar.

2. Mi madre insiste en que yo_____ (recoger) mi cuarto antes de salir.

3. Alejandro prefiere que ella _____ (conducir).

4. Espero que mis estudiantes _____ (venir) a verme a mi oficina hoy.

5. Tus padres quieren que tu _____ (construir) una casa cerca de la suya.

VERBS THAT END IN -CAR, -GAR, AND -ZAR

Some verbs have spelling changes in the subjunctive. These spelling changes are made to maintain the sound of the infinitive. If *tocar* became *toce*, the *c* would have an *s* sound, not the *k* sound it has in the infinitive. *G* followed by *e* in Spanish makes the *g* sound like an English *h*. *Gente. Generoso. Gu* keeps the hard *g* sound, as is *guerra, guerrilla.*

Verbs ending in *-car* change the *c-* to *qu*
    Example:

tocar—to touch, to play (the piano)

Singular	Plural
que yo toque	que nosotros toquemos
que tú toques	que vosotros toquéis
que él/ella/Ud. toque	que ellos/ellas/Uds. toquen

Other verbs like *tocar*:

   acercarse—to approach, to draw near

   buscar—to look for; to look up

chocar—to crash

colocar—to place

complicar—to complicate

comunicar—to communicate

criticar—to criticize

dedicar—to dedicate

educar—to educate

equivocarse—to make a mistake

EXERCISE 3.3

Give the present subjunctive of the regular verbs in the following sentences.

1. Mis padres esperan que sus hijos _____ (educarse) en buenas escuelas.

2. Temo que Uds. _____ (equivocarse).

3. A María no le gusta que Ud. la _____ (criticar) tanto.

4. Yo le exijo a mis estudiantes que _____ (buscar) las palabras nuevas en el diccionario.

5. Mi novia quiere que yo _____ (acercarse) a ella emocionalmente, pero soy muy reservado.

Verbs ending in -gar change the g to gu
Example:

pagar — to pay

Singular	Plural
que yo pague	que nosotros paguemos
que tú pagues	que vosotros paguéis
que él/ella/Ud. pague	que ellos/ellas/Uds. paguen

Other verbs like *pagar*:

tragar—to swallow

despegar—to take off (as a plane)

indagar—to question, interrogate

abogar –to advocate

pegar—to stick, to glue

Verbs ending in *-zar* change *z* to *c*

---

organizar—to organize

	Singular	Plural
	que yo organice	que nosotros organicemos
	que tú organices	que vosotros organicéis
	que él/ella/Ud. organice	que ellos/ellas/Uds. organicen

Other verbs like *organizar*:

calzar—to wear (as in shoe size)

almorzar—to have lunch

colonizar—to colonize

alcanzar—to reach

EXERCISE 3.4

Give the present subjunctive of the regular verbs in the following sentences.

1. Los pasajeros esperan que el Avión _____ (despegar) a tiempo.

2. Los indígenas temen que los extranjeros los _____ (colonizar).

3. Me imagino que José _____ (calzar) diez y medio.

4. La maestra quiere que sus alumnos _____ (pegar) las etiquetas en sus pupitres.

5. El contador insiste en que yo _____ (organizar) bien mis cuentas.

VERBS WITH STEM CHANGES IN THE PRESENT SUBJUNCTIVE

Stem-changing verbs that end in –ar maintain the regular conjugation in the *nosotros* and *vosotros* forms, but change *e* to *ie* in all the others. (Remember the "L" or "boot verbs" we reviewed earlier?)

confesar — to confess

Singular	Plural
que yo confiese	que nosotros confesemos
que tú confieses	que vosotros confeséis
que él/ella/Ud. confiese	que ellos/ellas/Uds. confiesen

Other verbs like *confesar:*

atraversar—to cross

comenzar—to begin

cruzar—to cross

despertar—to awaken

despertarse—to wake up

empezar—to begin

encerrar—to enclose; to lock in

negar—to deny

nevar—to snow

pensar—to think

recomendar—to recommend

sentarse—to sit down

temblar—to tremble

EXERCISE 3.5

Give the present subjunctive of the verbs in the following sentences.

1. Espero que ellos _____ (despertar) a José a eso de las ocho de la mañana.

2. Yo quiero que Uds. _____ (sentirse) como en su casa.

3. El cura quiere que yo _____ (confesarse) antes de tomar la comunión.

4. No entiendo que ellos _____ (negar) lo que han hecho.

5. Parece increíble que el metro _____ (atravesar) la ciudad tan rápidamente.

Verbs ending in –er, maintain the regular conjugation in the *nosotros* and *vosotros* forms, but *e* changes to *ie* in all the others.

---

querer—to want, to wish, to love (a person)

Singular	Plural
que yo quiera	que nosotros queramos
que tú quieras	que vosotros queráis
que él/ella/Ud. quiera	que ellos/ellas/Uds. quieran

Example:

¡No me importa lo que él quiera!
I don't care what he wants!

Other verbs like *querer*:

defender—to defend

encender—to light, to ignite; to turn on (a lamp)

entender—to understand

perder—to lose

Verbs ending in –ir, change *e* to *i* in the *nosotros* and *vosotros* forms, but *e* to *ie* in the all the others.

---

preferir—to prefer

Singular	Plural
que yo prefiera	que nosotros prefiramos
que tú prefieras	que vosotros prefiráis
que él/ella/Ud. prefiera	que ellos/ellas/Uds. prefieran

Other verbs like *preferir*:

mentir—to lie

divertir—to amuse

divertirse—to amuse oneself; to enjoy oneself

sentir—to regret

sentirse—to feel (sick, better, etc.)

EXERCISE 3.6

Give the present subjunctive of the verbs in the following sentences.

1. Espero que ellos _____ (divertirse) mucho en la fiesta.

2. No creo que Uds. _____ (sentirse) bien aquí; hace mucho frío.

3. Dudo que él _____ (querer) despertarse antes de las 8 de la mañana.

4. Ojalá que mis profesoras no _____ (querer) dar clases hoy.

5. Me importa mucho que vosotros _____ (divertirse) en los Estados Unidos.

Stem-changing verbs (*o* to *ue*)

Verbs ending in –*ar*, maintain the regular conjugation in the *nosotros* and *vosotros* forms, but change to *ue* in all the others.

jugar—to play

Singular	Plural
que yo **juegue**	que nosotros **juguemos**
que tú **juegues**	que vosotros **juguéis**
que él ella/Ud. **juegue**	que ellos/ellas/Uds. **jueguen**

Other verbs like *jugar*:

acordarse (de)—to remember

acostar—to put to bed

acostarse—to go to bed; to lay down

almorzar—to have lunch

costar—to cost

contar—to count

demostrar—to demonstrate

encontrar—to find

encontrarse (con)—to meet

mostrar—to show

probar—to try; to taste

probarse—to try on (a garment)

recordar—to remember

rogar—to beg

sonar—to sound; to ring

soñar—to dream

volar—to fly

EXERCISE 3.7

Give the present subjunctive of the verbs in the following sentences.

1. Es posible que ellos _____ (almorzar) en casa de su abuela.

2. Es conveniente que Uds. _____ (probarse) los zapatos antes de comprárselos.

3. Dudo que don Pedro _____ (volar) con esa aerolínea.

4. Se requiere que los estudiantes _____ (demostrar) todo lo que han aprendido.

5. Es poco probable que yo _____ (encontrar) ese libro en esta librería.

Stem changing verbs ending in –er maintain the regular conjugation in the *nosotros* and *vosotros* forms, but change *o* to *ue* in all the other forms.

volver—to return, to go back

Singular	Plural
que yo **vuelva**	que nosotros **volvamos**
que tú **vuelvas**	que vosotros **volváis**
que él/ella/Ud. **vuelva**	que ellos/ellas/Uds. **vuelvan**

Other verbs like *volver*:

   devolver—to return; to give back

   doler—to hurt; to ache

   envolver—to wrap

   llover—to rain

   mover—to move

   poder—to be able

EXERCISE 3.8
Give the present subjunctive of the verbs in the following sentence fragments.

1. No creo que ellos _____ (poder) entregarme el trabajo antes del 23 de enero.

2. Necesito que Uds. _____ (mover) la mesa hacia el lado de la puerta.

3. Es probable que _____ (llover) esta tarde.

4. Quiere que ellas _____ (envolver) los regalos con este papel.

5. La bibliotecaria insiste en que yo _____ (devolver) el libro esta semana.

IRREGULAR FORMS IN THE SUBJUNCTIVE
Some verbs are irregular in the subjunctive. These verbs are also irregular in the *yo* form in the present indicative; the *yo* form does not end in *o*. Look at the following examples.

dar — to give

Singular	Plural
que yo dé	que nosotros demos
que tú des	que vosotros deis
que él/ella/Ud. dé	que ellos/ellas/Uds. den

estar — to be

Singular	Plural
que yo esté	que nosotros estemos
que tú estés	que vosotros estéis
que él/ella/Ud esté	que ellos/ellas/Uds. estén

ir — to go

Singular	Plural
que yo vaya	que nosotros vayamos
que tú vayas	que vosotros vayáis
que él/ella/Ud. vaya	que ellos/ellas/Uds. vayan

saber — to know

Singular	Plural
que yo sepa	que nosotros sepamos
que tú sepas	que vosotros sepáis
que él/ella/Ud. sepa	que ellos/ellas/Uds. sepan

ser — to be

Singular	Plural
que yo sea	que nosotros seamos
que tú seas	que vosotros seáis
que él/ella/Ud. sea	que ellos/ellas/Uds. sean

haber — to have

Singular	Plural
que yo haya	que nosotros hayamos
que tú hayas	que vosotros hayáis
que él/ella/Ud. haya	que ellos/ellas/Uds. hayan

Haber—to have (helping verb used to form the compound tenses)
Use *haber* + past participle.

Examples:

Espero que Pedro **haya regresado** a su casa.

Mis padres se alegran de **que yo haya venido** a visitarlos.

Me fascina **que tú hayas ganado** este premio.

Dudo **que él haya tenido** que trabajar hoy.

La profesora se alegra de **que nosotros hayamos sacado** tan buenas notas.

Es increíble **que vosotros hayáis gastado** tanto dinero.

Espero **que ellos hayan encontrado** el edificio sin mucha dificultad.

EXERCISE 3.9

The psychotherapist talks about his hopelessly romantic patient, José, who suffers from "unrequited love sydrome." Fill in the blanks using the present subjunctive for the verbs indicated.

José quiere que María _____ (**ser**) su mujer, pero ella no lo quiere. El desea que ella _____ (**estar**) a su lado para siempre y le _____ (**dar**) muchos hijos. María le ha dicho que no, pero él insiste en que ella _____ (**ir**) con él hasta el fin del mundo. Y aunque ella le diga que no iría ni hasta la esquina con él, él insiste en que ella _____ (**saber**) cuánto la quiere para que cambie de idea. Temo que José padezca del terrible síndrome de Don Quijote.

Here are some verbs that require the subjunctive in the dependent clause. Since the subjunctive has to do with influence, they are broken up here into categories of influence, to make it a bit easier.

Expressions used to solicit and give orders

querer que—to wish

exigir que—to demand; to require

insistir en que—to insist

mandar que—to order

pedir que—to ask; to request

rogar que—to beg; to pray

suplicar que—to beg; to implore

Examples:

> Quiero que los Mets ganen la Serie Mundial.
> *I want the Mets to win the World Series.*
>
> La universidad exige que guardemos silencio después de las diez.
> *The university demands that we be quiet after 10 o'clock.*

Expressions used to convey desire

desear que—to desire; to wish

esperar que—to hope

ojalá que—let's hope that

Examples:

> Ojalá que nos ganemos la lotería.
> *I hope we win the lottery.*
>
> Deseo que mi hija estudie en Princeton.
> *I want my daughter to study in Princeton.*

Expressions used to give advice

aconsejar que—to advise

recomendar que—to recommend

sugerir que—to suggest

permitir que—to permit

Examples:

> El cirujano me aconseja que me haga la operación lo más pronto posible.
> *The surgeon recommends I have the operation as soon as possible.*
>
> Mis amigos me aconsejan que deje de fumar.
> *My friends advise me to quit smoking.*

Expressions used to give permission

dejar que—to let

permitir que—to let; to allow

impedir que—to prevent

oponerse a que—to be against; opposed to

prohibir que—to forbid

Examples:

> Los gobiernos represivos no permiten que sus ciudadanos se expresen libremente.
>
> *Oppresive governments do not let their citizens express themselves freely.*

Expressions used to convey skepticism, doubt, uncertainty, disbelief and denial

dudar que—to doubt that

no creer que—to not believe that

no pensar que—to not think that

no estar seguro de que—to not be sure that

negar que—to deny that

no es verdad que—it is not true that

puede ser que—it could be that

Examples:

> Dudo que los estudiantes estén contentos con las notas.
> *I doubt the students are happy with their grades.*

> No creo que José sepa que estamos aquí.
> *I do not believe José knows (that) we are here.*

IMPERSONAL EXPRESSIONS

The subjunctive is used after certain impersonal expressions that show necessity, doubt, regret, importance, urgency, or possibility.

es absurdo que—it is absurd that

es agradable que—it is pleasant that

es bueno que—it is good that

es dudoso que—it is doubtful that

es escandaloso que—it is scandalous that

es importante que—it is important that

es imposible que—it is impossible that

es improbable que—it is improbable that

es justo que—it is fair that

es malo que—it is bad that

es necesario que—it is necessary that

es posible que—it is possible that

es preciso que—it is necessary that

es poco probable que—it is unlikely that

es raro que—it is strange that

es ridículo que—it is ridiculous that

es sorprendente que—it is surprising that

es una lástima que—it is a shame that

vale la pena que—it is worth the trouble

Es escandaloso que la compañía de teléfono nos cobre tanto.

It is scandalous that the telephone company charges us so much.

No vale la pena que vengan a la fiesta. No está muy buena.

It's not worth your coming to the party. It's not very good.

EXERCISE 3.10

Look at the following examples:

En algunos países los hombres pueden tener más de una esposa legalmente.

In some countries men are allowed to have more than one wife legally.

No creo que sea justo que algunos hombres puedan tener más de una esposa.

I do not think that it is fair that some men can have more than one wife.

Hay millones de personas sin seguro médico en los EEUU.

There are millions of people without medical insurance in the U.S.

Es increíble que haya miles de personas sin seguro médico en los EEUU.

It is incredible that there are millions of people without medical insurance in the U.S.

Express your opinion about the following, using one of the impersonal expressions.

1. Las mujeres ganan menos que los hombres.

2. Los estadounidenses son fanáticos del fútbol americano.

3. La Internet ofrece una enorme cantidad de información.

4. El número de divorcios aumenta (increases) cada año.

EXERCISE 3.11

Use your logic. Match up the elements of each column to create logical sentences. The Column B verbs will be in the present indicative and the Column D verbs will be in the present subjunctive.

EXAMPLE: El médico recomienda que el paciente tome la píldora para la hipertensión.

Column A	Column B
el médico	querer
el psicólogo	preferir
los estudiantes	necesitar
la madre	sugerir
el chofer	recomendar

Column C	Column D
la profesora	ponerse el vestido rosado.
el paciente	hacer ejercicios.
el cliente	hablar acerca de su niñez traumática.
el pasajero	escribir tres párrafos sobre el tema.
la hija	cerrar la ventanilla del carro.

Since the subjunctive is used to express emotions, it would follow logically that it would be used in exclamations of emotion. Here are some of the exclamations.

¡Qué bueno!—Great!

¡Qué estupendo!—Fantastic!

¡Qué maravilloso!—Marvelous!

¡Qué horrible!—What a horrible thing!

¡Qué malo!—Too bad!

¡Qué triste!—How sad!

¡Qué extraño!—How strange!

¡Qué raro!—How odd!

¡Qué alegría!—It's great!

¡Qué felicidad!—I'm so happy!

¡Qué lástima!—What a pity!

¡Qué pena!—How sad!

¡Qué vergüenza!—What a shame!

¡Qué tristeza!—How sad!

¡Qué sorpresa!—What a surprise!

Examples:

Tus primos llegan de Caracas mañana.

> ¡Qué estupendo! ¡Qué bueno!
> *Your cousins arrive from Caracas tomorrow.*
> *How wonderful! Great!*

Todos los pasajeros murieron en el accidente.

> ¡Qué horrible! ¡Qué triste!
> *All the passengers died in the accident.*
> *How horrible! How sad!*

These expressions can also be followed by the subjunctive in a sentence: exclamation + *que* + subject + verb in the subjunctive.

> ¡Qué bueno que no tengas que ir a la reunión! Ahora podrás venir a la fiesta.
> *How great that you don't have to go to the meeting! Now you can come to the party.*

> ¡Qué pena que sea tan antipático tu jefe!
> *What a shame that your boss is so unpleasant!*

> ¡Qué lástima que José tenga que trabajar mañana.
> *What a shame that José has to work tomorrow!*

EXERCISE 3.12

Write the correct form of the verb in parentheses.

1. ¡Qué estupendo que Uds. _____ (estar) aquí!

2. ¡Qué malo que María y yo no _____ (poder) asistir a la boda!

3. ¡Qué raro que tú _____ (tener) que irte tan temprano!

4. ¡Qué lástima que Julia _____ (querer) acompañarnos!

5. ¡Qué tristeza que sus padres no _____ (saber) nada de ella!

The present subjunctive follows an expression of personal feeling when:

1. There is more than one subject.

   (Yo) necesito que (tú) vengas conmigo.
   I need you to come with me.

2. The emotions are felt at the moment they are expressed.

   Me alegro de que estés aquí conmigo.
   I am happy you are here with me.

3. What is being reacted to occurs at the same time or is expected to occur after the feelings are expressed.

   Esperamos que el vuelo llegue a tiempo.
   We hope the flight arrives on time.

   Es recomendable que (tú) veas al médico mañana.
   It is advisable that you see the doctor tomorrow.

There are impersonal expressions that express certainty.

   Es cierto que Ricky Martin hizo telenovelas norte-americanas.
   It is true that Ricky Martin worked in American soap operas.

   No es evidente que mi cliente sea inocente.
   It is not obvious that my client is innocent.

In the affirmative, these statements communicate definite truths, at least from the point of view of the speaker. In the negative, they are treated as opinion and require the subjunctive.

Es cierto que él es culpable.
It is true that he is guilty.

No es cierto que él sea culpable.
It is not true that he is guilty.

Es obvio que Lena tiene la razón.
It is obvious that Lena is right.

No es obvio que Lena tenga la razón.
It is not obvious that Lena is right.

Es seguro que los niños llegan hoy
It is definite that the children arrive today.

No es seguro que los niños lleguen hoy.
It is not definite that the children will arrive today.

FORMATION

Impersonal expression of certainty + *que* + subject + verb in the indicative.

Note: The verb in the indicative can be in the present, preterit, or imperfect.

Es obvio que José nunca quiso a María.
It is obvious that José never loved María.

Es verdad que los romanos construían buenas carreteras.
It is true that the Romans used to construct great highways.

No es verdad que José esté muy enfermo ¿no?
It's not true that José is very ill, right?

No es seguro que haya cupo en el vuelo.
It's not definite that there be a seat on the flight.

EXPRESSIONS OF EMOTION

alegrarse de que—to become (be made) happy

enorgullecerse de—to be proud of

lamentar—to regret

molestarse—to get upset; annoyed

enfadarse—to get angry

temer que—to fear

tener miedo (de) que—to be afraid

sorprenderse que—to be surprised

emocionarse que—to be moved; to get excited

> Me emociona que vengas a visitarme.
> *I am excited that you are coming to visit me.*

> Tememos que los estudiantes estén en peligro.
> *We fear that the students may be in danger.*

> Lamentan que su caso no se pueda resolver este año.
> *They regret that your case cannot be resolved this year.*

It is also possible to convey feelings and emotions regarding an action or state with the construction:

estar/ser + adjective that conveys emotion + *de que* + subjunctive

For example,

> Estoy contenta de que estés aquí con tu familia.
> *I am happy that you are here with your family.*

> No estamos seguros de que sepas llegar hasta allá.
> *We are not sure you know how to get there.*

Some adjectives that can be used in this construction are:

alegre—happy

contento—happy

encantado—delighted

desilusionado—disillusioned; disappointed

enfadado/a—angry

triste—sad

orgulloso—proud

Examples:

> Estoy muy orgulloso de que te hayas graduado de la Universidad de Harvard.
> *I am very proud that you have graduated from Harvard.*

> Estamos encantados de que vengas a visitarnos.
> *We are so glad that they come to visit us.*

> Es decepcionante que no puedan conseguir entradas para el concierto de Ricky Martin.
> *It's disappointing that they are not able to get tickets for the Ricky Martin concert.*

PRESENT PERFECT SUBJUNCTIVE

To express feelings or attitudes about past occurrences that are felt at the moment they are expressed, Spanish speakers use the present perfect subjunctive.

> Siento que no hayas visto la exposición de Mario.
> *I am sorry you did not see Mario's exhibition.*

> Espero que te haya gustado la película.
> *I hope you liked the film.*

FORMATION

The present perfect subjunctive is formed using the present subjunctive of *haber* + past participle of the verb.

Que yo haya	venido (venir)
Que tú hayas	bailado (bailar)
Que él/ella/Ud. se haya	desayunado (desayunarse)
Que nosotros hayamos	sido (ser)
Que vosotros hayáis	esperado (esperar)
Que ellos/ellas/Uds. hayan	salido (salir)

El detective duda que María haya cometido el asesinato.
The detective doubts that María committed the murder.

Espero que mi equipaje haya llegado.
I hope my luggage arrived.

Lamento que no te hayan ofrecido el puesto.
I'm sorry they didn't offer you the position.

No creemos que José y María hayan cometido un delito.
We don't believe that José and María committed a crime.

Remember, when using the present perfect subjunctive, you need:

1. to have two different subjects, the second one being in the present perfect subjunctive
2. what is being reacted to has already occurred

EXERCISE 3.13
Provide the present perfect subjunctive in the following sentences.

1. Estoy contento de que los Yankees _____ (ganar) la Serie Mundial.

2. Me parece extraño que Marta no _____ (venir) a la escuela hoy.

3. Temo que mis amigos _____ (perderse) en la carretera.

4. Nos hace ilusión que Uds. _____ (decidir) ir a Buenos Aries con nosotras.

5. ¡Qué romántico que tú le _____ (traer) rosas a María!

EXPRESSING FEELINGS ABOUT PAST EVENTS
The imperfect subjunctive is used to express the same types of ideas as the present subjunctive but in reference to the past. So it makes total sense that it is used with the same expressions (wish or desire, emotion, impersonal expressions), but with the *past* tense.

Look at these examples:

Present Subjunctive

Queremos que **gane** el otro candidato.
We want the other candidate to win.

Espera que te **gusten** sus frijoles.
He hopes you like his beans.

Necesito que el médico me **vea** inmediatamente.
It is necessary that the doctor see me immediately.

Quieren que **vayas** a su fiesta de despedida.
They want you to go to their going away party.

Imperfect Subjunctive

Queríamos que **ganara** el otro candidato.
We wanted the other candidate to win.

Esperaba que te **gustaran** sus frijoles.
He hoped you would like his beans.

Necesitaba que el médico me **viera** inmediatamente.
It was necessary that the doctor see me immediately.

Querían que **fueras** a su fiesta de despedida.
They wanted you to go to their going away party.

Dudo que **lleguen** a tiempo.
I doubt they'll arrive on time.

Dudaba que **llegaran** a tiempo.
I doubted they would arrive on time.

FORMATION OF THE IMPERFECT SUBJUNCTIVE

Good news! The imperfect subjunctive is the easiest of the past tenses of the subjunctive.

To form the imperfect subjunctive, take the *ellos* form of the preterit minus the *-ron*, then add the imperfect endings. (Note: The *nosotros* form calls for a written accent.)

hablar — to talk

Singular	Plural
que yo hablara	que nosotros habláramos
que tú hablaras	que vosotros hablarais
que él/ella/Ud. hablara	que ellos/ellas/Uds. hablaran
or	
que yo hablase	que nosotros hablásemos
que tú hablases	que vosotros hablaseis
que él/ella/Ud. hablase	que ellos/ellas/Uds. hablasen

comer — to eat

Singular	Plural
que yo comiera	que nosotros comiéramos
que tú comieras	que vosotros comierais
que él/ella/Ud. comiera	que ellos/ellas/Uds. comieran
or	
que yo comiese	que nosotros comiésemos
que tú comieses	que vosotros comieseis
que él/ella/Ud. comiese	que ellos/ellas/Uds. comiesen

vivir — to live

Singular	Plural
que yo viviera	que nosotros viviéramos
que tú vivieras	que vosotros vivierais
que él/ella/Ud. viviera	que ellos/ellas/Uds. vivieran
or	
que yo viviese	que nosotros viviésemos
que tú vivieses	que vosotros vivieseis
que él/ella/Ud. viviese	que ellos/ellas/Uds. viviesen

The above examples are with regular preterit verbs. This formation, however, applies to all verbs, be they regular or irregular, in the preterit. *Ir* for example is irregular in the preterit.

The third person plural of *ir* is *fueron*. Following the rule, the imperfect subjunctive stem becomes *fue* + *-ra, -ras, -ra, -ramos, -rais, -ran*.

EXERCISE 3.14

The following verbs are irregular. Write the *ellos* form of the verb in the preterit in the first column and the *yo* form in the imperfect subjunctive in the second.

Infinitive	Preterite	Imperfect Subjunctive
1. andar	1.	1.
2. dar	2.	2.
3. dormir	3.	3.
4. hacer	4.	4.
5. ir	5.	5.
6. leer	6.	6.
7. poder	7.	7.
8. querer	8.	8.
9. ser	9.	9.
10. traer	10.	10.

USES OF THE IMPERFECT SUBJUNCTIVE

The imperfect subjunctive is used in a subordinate clause when the main clause verb is the past and requires subjunctive mood.

¿Qué quería Isabel?

Quería que yo **fuera** a su casa.

What did Isabel want?

She wanted me to go to her house.

Quería is the verb of the main clause. It is in the past tense and requires the subjunctive mood. *Fuera* is the verb of the dependent clause. It is in the imperfect subjunctive.

¿Qué te dijo el médico?

Me recomendó que tomara esta medicina.

What did the doctor say?

He recommended I take this medicine.

The imperfect subjunctive is also used when the main clause verb is in the present, but the dependent clause refers to the past.

Es una lástima que no fueras conmigo.
It's a shame you didn't go with me.

Es impresionante que supieras hablar inglés a esa edad.
It's impressive that you know how to speak English at that age.

The imperfect subjunctive of *querer* (*quisiera*) is used to make a request politely.

Quisiera saber si está Rachel.
I would like to know if Rachel is here.

Quisiéramos comprar este refrigerador.
We would like to buy this refrigerator.

EXERCISE 3.15
José and María talk about the party they had last night. Complete the sentences with the imperfect subjunctive of the verb indicated.

1. Nos alegró que la gente _____ (disfrutar) tanto en la fiesta.

2. Fue una suerte que tu madre _____ (preparar) tanta comida casera.

3. Teníamos miedo de que el equipo de música no _____ (funcionar).

4. Sentí mucho que algunos compañeros de trabajo no _____. (venir)

5. Los invitados estaban contentos de que Tony _____ (ocuparse) de la música.

"IF" CLAUSES

The *imperfect subjunctive* is also used in *if* clauses with contrary to fact and hypothetical statements. The verb in the result clause would be in the conditional.

Let's break this down.

> Si yo fuera Ud. ...
> *If I were you ...*

> Si yo fuera Manuel, tomaría dos semanas de vacaciones.
> *If I were Manuel, I would take a two-week vacation.*

> Si no hiciera tanto frío, iría a trotar.
> *If it weren't so cold out, I would go jogging.*

If there is a possibility that the situation will happen, the *if* clause calls for the indicative. The present subjunctive is *never* used in an *if* clause.

> Vamos a acampar si no llueve.
> *We are going camping if it doesn't rain.*

> Si me gano la lotería, me voy a comprar una casa de campo.
> *If I win the lottery, I am going to buy a house in the country.*

EXERCISE 3.16

Complete the following dialogue, using the imperfect subjunctive.

1. Si el banco _____ (bajar) los intereses, nuestros clientes solicitarían un mayor número de préstamos.

2. Si _____ (ser) tan rica como Madonna, le regalaría un avión privado a mi familia.

3. Si José le _____ (prestar) más atención a sus hijos, éstos no serían tan problemáticos en la escuela.

4. ¡Yo sería el hombre más contento del mundo si Carmen _____ (casarse) conmigo!

5. Mi vida cambiaría por completo si _____ (tener) que trasladarme a otro país.

PAST PERFECT SUBJUNCTIVE

To express feeling and doubts or uncertainties that were felt in the past about events that took place BEFORE the action of the main verb (that is the verb in the dependent clause), use the past perfect subjunctive.

> Temí que mis estudiantes no hubieran comprendido la lección.
>
> *I feared that my students had not understood the lesson.*

> El detective dudaba que María hubiera cometido el asesinato.
>
> *The detective doubted that María had committed the murder.*

> Nos alegramos de que te hubieras ganado la beca.
>
> *We were happy that you had gotten the scholarship.*

FORMATION

To form the past perfect subjunctive, simply conjugate *haber* in the imperfect subjunctive and add the past participle.

For example:

que yo hubiera cenado (cenar)

que tú hubieras estado (estar)

que él/ella/Ud hubiera ido (ir)

que nosotros hubiéramos bailado (bailar)

que vosotros hubierais salido (salir)

que ellos/ellas/Uds. hubieran cantado (cantar)

NOTE: Remember that both the present perfect subjunctive and the past perfect subjunctive are used to describe actions that have occurred before the main clause verb.

The past perfect subjunctive is used when the main clause verb is in a past tense (preterit, imperfect, past perfect) or the past conditional. Look at these examples.

The main clause verb is in the *preterit*:

> Me **pareció** tan lamentable que no *hubieran podido* escapar del incendio.
>
> *I thought it was so sad that they weren't able to escape the blaze.*

The main clause verb is in the *imperfect:*

> ¡**Era** imposible que ellos *hubieran sido* los culpables!
>
> *It was impossible that they would have been guilty.*

The main clause verb is in the *past perfect:*

> Yo siempre **había dudado** de que ella *hubiera tomado* el collar.
>
> *I had always doubted that she had taken the necklace.*

The main clause verb is in the past *conditional:*

> **Habría** sido una lástima que Uds. no *hubieran conocido* a mis parientes.
>
> *It would have been a shame if you had not met my relatives.*

EXERCISE 3.17

Tell how the following people responded to these events in the past. Use the context of the sentences to determine which expression is required in the independent clause. For example, if disappointment is the logical reaction, you might use *lamentar que*. Put the dependent clause verb in the *past perfect subjunctive.*

Examples:

> Mario tomó su examen. Supe que había sacado una buena nota.
>
> *Mario took his exam. I found out that he had gotten a good grade.*
>
> Me alegré de que Mario hubiera sacado una buena nota en su examen.
>
> *I was happy that Mario had gotten a good grade on his exam.*

1. Los aficionados de los Mets esperaban que su equipo ganara la Serie Mundial. Los Mets no la ganaron.
2. Mi hermano fue de vacaciones a Puerto Rico. Conoció a Chayanne, el cantante.
3. Miguel fue a ver una película. Esperaba que el protagonista sobreviviera. El protagonista murió.
4. La policía acusó a mi hijo de un delito. Mi hijo me aseguró de que era inocente.

The following conjuctions, when used to express a future action, take the present subjunctive. Why? Because the completion of the actions, events, or situations in the time clause is uncertain.

antes de que—before

cuando—when

después (de) que—afterward

en cuanto—as soon as

hasta que—until

mientras—while

tan pronto como—as soon as

Examples:

Planificaremos la función cuando recibamos los fondos.

We will plan the event when we receive the funds.

Estaremos en el aeropuerto dos horas antes de que salga el avión.

We will be at the airport two hours before the flight leaves.

José nos llamará en cuanto llegue a México.

José will call us as soon as he arrives in Mexico.

Después de que nos casemos, nos trasladaremos a Bogotá, Colombia.

After we get married, we will move to Bogota, Colombia.

Los Congresistas levantarán el embargo en cuanto el pueblo estadounidense exprese su desacuerdo.

Congress will lift the embargo as soon as the people of the United States express their disapproval.

Notice here Congress will do something when a certain condition occurs. Will that condition be met? The probability is high, at least from the speaker's point of view.

EXERCISE 3.18

María talks about what she will do when she gets to "La Gran Manzana" (The Big Apple). Give the subjunctive of the verbs in parentheses.

Tan pronto como me ____1____ (graduarse) de la universidad este año, iré a Nueva York a empezar mi carrera profesional como actriz de Broadway. En cuanto ____2____ (llegar) a la Gran Manzana, me matricularé en clases de baile, danza y actuación. Mientras ____3____ (tomar) mis clases, me presentaré a todas las audiciones hasta que ____4____ (lograr) un papel en alguna obra de Broadway. Cuando ____5____ (tener) un papel principal y ____6____ (ser) la estrella, seré famosa.

SUBJUNCTIVE AFTER *ANTES DE QUE*

Antes de que always requires the subjunctive because the action it introduces is always future in relation to the action of the main verb.

> Los alumnos entregarán sus exámenes antes de que la profesora hable con el director.
>
> *The students will hand in their exams before the teacher talks to the principal.*

Remember that when there is no change in subject, *antes de que* is always followed by the infinitive.

> Los músicos ensayaron durante tres meses antes de presentarse en Carnegie Hall.
>
> *The musicians rehearsed for three months before performing at Carnegie Hall.*

> George Washington fue soldado antes de ser presidente.
>
> *George Washington was a soldier before he was president.*

Certain conjunctions introduce clauses that establish a restriction on an action. Since the actions, events, or situations that these conjunctions introduce may not take place, they are always followed by the subjunctive.

Some common conjunctions of this type are:

a menos que—unless

con tal (de) que—provided that

sin que—without

en caso de que—in case

> Las leyes no cambiarán a menos que el público se manifieste en contra de ellas.
>
> *The laws will not change unless the public protests against them.*

> Yo te los mandaré con tal de que me des la dirección exacta.
>
> *I will send them to you provided you give me the exact address.*

> Nosotros no iremos a la fiesta sin que nos pongamos de acuerdo anteriormente.
>
> *We won't go to the party without having coordinated things beforehand.*

> El abogado llamará a la Sra. Díaz en caso de que necesite otro testigo.
>
> *The lawyer will call on Mrs. Díaz should he need another witness.*

Remember that the infinitive is used after the preposition *sin* when there is no change in subject.

> Nunca salgo sin cerrar la puerta con llave.
>
> *I never go out without locking the door.*

Certain conjunctions express the purpose or intention of an action. Some of the most common are:

a fin de que—in order that

para que—in order that

de manera que—so as, so that

de modo que—so as, so that

1. Los jefes estimulan a los empleados de modo que sean más productivos.

   Bosses encourage their employees so that they are more productive.

2. Los estudiantes se manifestaron para que los Congresistas tomaran conciencia del problema.

The students protested to make Congress aware of the problem.

Remember: If both verbs share the same subject, the preposition *para* is used followed by the infinitive.

Nosotros escuchamos la radio para saber las noticias.

We listen to the radio in order to know the news.

Here the plot thickens yet some more! Let's look at when we need the subjunctive as opposed to the indicative with the conjunction *aunque*.

When *aunque* is followed by the subjunctive it means "even if" and expresses doubt or uncertainty about whether an action, event, or situation is going to happen.

Aunque tenga mil cosas que hacer, te llamaré esta tarde.

Even if I have a thousand things to do, I will call you this afternoon.

When *aunque* is followed by the indicative, it means "even though" or "although" and presents actions, events or situations as established facts.

Aunque tengo mil cosas que hacer, voy a llamar a María.

Even though I have a thousand things to do, I am going to call María.

GIVING COMMANDS

You can also affect the behavior of others by directly telling them what you want them to do. You can be either formal or informal in Spanish when "bossing" others around. Let's take a look at formal commands first, since they look exactly like the present subjunctive.

These are examples of formal commands.

Hable (Ud.) con José.
Talk to José.

No hable (Ud.) en clase.
Do not speak in class.

Regresen (Uds.) a tiempo.
Get back on time. (plural)

Devuelvan (Uds.) los videos al Blockbusters.
Return the videos to Blockbusters. (plural)

No pongan (Uds.) los bolsos en el piso.
Do not put the pocketbooks on the floor.

Note: In formal commands you are politely telling one or more persons to do something. The pronouns *Ud.* and *Uds.* can be, but are rarely used in Spanish. When they are used, it is usually for emphasis.

FORMATION

To form a formal command with an *-ar* verb, follow the pattern for the subjunctive.

1. Determine the present indicative of the verb. Let's work with *hablar. Yo hablo.*

2. Drop the *yo* pronoun and change the *-o* to *-e* because the infinitive ends in *-ar*.

3. Add *-en* to create the plural formal command.

    Hable (Ud.) *Hablen* (Uds.)

For *-er* and *-ir* verbs:

1. Determine the *yo* form of the present indicative of the verb. Let's see *beber. Yo bebo.*

2. Drop the *yo* pronoun and change the *-o* to *-a* because the infinitive ends in *-er*.

    Add *-an* to create the plural formal command.
    Beba (Ud.) Beban (Uds.)

    For *-ir*, let's use *vivir.*

1. Determine the *yo* form of the present indicative of the verb. *Yo vivo.*

2. Drop the *yo* and change the *-o* to *-a*.

3. Add *-an* to create the plural.

    Viva (Ud.) Vivan (Uds.)

EXERCISE 3.19

Give the present indicative, then the singular and plural formal commands for the following verbs.

Infinitive
1.   comer
2.   estudiar
3.   caminar
4.   decidir
5.   cambiar

Present indicative for *yo*
1.   _____
2.   _____
3.   _____
4.   _____
5.   _____

Ud. command
1.   _____
2.   _____
3.   _____
4.   _____
5.   _____

Uds. command
1.   _____
2.   _____
3.   _____
4.   _____
5.   _____

You can also give commands that include the speaker. You would use the *nosotros* form.

¡Bailemos!

Let's dance!

¡No discutamos!

Let's not argue!

¡Salgamos!

Let's go out!

¡No salgamos!

Let's not go out!

There are some verbs that are irregular in the imperative.

Dar: dé

Ir: vaya

Ser: sea

Saber: sepa

Examples:

> Estamos recogiendo dinero para la lucha contra el SIDA. Dé lo que pueda.
> *We are raising money for the fight against AIDS. Please give what you can.*

> Vaya con Dios.
> *Go with God.*

> Sepan que los queremos mucho.
> *Know we love you very much.*

> Hágase médico o abogado. Ambas son profesiones muy bien pagadas.
> *Become a doctor or a lawyer. Both are well-paying professions.*

GIVING INFORMAL COMMANDS

The form used to give informal commands is the same as the *él/ella* form in the present indicative, with a few exceptions, of course!

There are times when the main clause is dropped to give an indirect command. The subjunctive clause stands alone, yet the main verb is understood.

When a Spaniard cries out, "*¡Que viva España!*" (Live Spain) he/she is really saying "*Quiero que viva España.*" (I want Spain to live.) *Quiero que* is understood.

Look at these examples:

> Doctor, la Sra. Ramos lo está esperando.
> *Doctor, Mrs. Ramos is waiting.*

> ¡Que pase inmediamente!
> *Have her come in immediately!*

El Presidente Clinton necesita hablar con Ud.
President Clinton wants to talk to you.

¡Que espere!
Let him wait!

Look at these two sentences:

María compra la leche en el supermercado.
María buys milk at the supermarket.

María, si vas al supermercado, compra leche.
Maria, if you go to the supermarket, buy milk.

The negative informal command is the same as the second-person singular of the present subjunctive.

No seas estúpido.
Don't be stupid.

No mastiques con la boca abierta.
Don't chew with your mouth open.

Here are some irregular verbs in the informal command form and their roots.

poner (and its derivatives *suponer, posponer, etc*): **pon**

Pon el abrigo en el armario.
Put the coat in the closet.

salir (*sobresalir*): **sal**

Sal conmigo esta noche.
Go out with me tonight.

tener (*mantener, sostener*): **ten**

Ten cuidado.
Be careful.

venir (*intervienir, prevenier*): **ven**

Ven a casa a las diez.
Come to my house at ten.

hacer (*satisfacer*): **haz**

Haz la tarea ahora mismo.

Do your homework right now.

decir: di

¡Dime la verdad! ¿Por qué no viniste anoche?

Tell me the truth! Why didn't you come last night?

ser: sé

Sé más amistoso con la gente.

Be friendlier with people.

ir: ve

Ve a ver al médico esta tarde.

Go see the doctor this afternoon.

EXERCISE 3.20

Write the informal affirmative command.

María tells her daughter what to do while she is away.

1. _____ atención a tu abuela. (prestarle)

2. _____ la tarea en cuanto regreses a casa. (hacer)

3. _____ el piano todos los días. (practicar)

4. _____ la mesa a la hora de comer. (poner)

5. _____ la ropa blanca con lejía. (lavar)

When addressing more than one person in the informal *vosotros*, or *vosotras*, drop the *r* of the infinitive and add -*d*. Remember, the *vosotros* form is not as commonly used as *Uds.*

Examples:

Hablad con ellos.

Talk to them.

Caminad por el centro de la ciudad.

Walk around the city's downtown.

To form the negative imperative, use the same form as the second-person plural of the present subjunctive.

No habléis.

Don't talk.

When addressing someone informally, tell them not to do something by putting *no* in front of the *tú* and *vosotros* forms of the present subjunctive.

No seas tan testarudo.

Don't be so hard-headed.

¡No me hables en ese tono de voz!

Don't talk to me with this tone of voice.

No cambies más de idea.

Don't change your mind again.

No digas que no te previne.

Don't say (that) I didn't warn you.

DIRECT AND INDIRECT OBJECT PRONOUNS WITH COMMAND FORMS

Direct and indirect object pronouns can be attached to imperatives. Let's look at direct object pronouns first.

Whenever you make an affirmative command, the object pronouns are attached at the end of the verb, forming a single word.

¿Dónde pongo el dinero?

Póngalo en el mostrador.

Where do I put the money?

Put it on the counter

¿Quieres que invite a María a tu fiesta?

¡Sí, por supuesto! Invítala de mi parte.

Do you want me to invite María to your party?

Of course! Invite her on my behalf.

¿Cuándo compro las flores?

Cómprelas mañana.

When do I buy the flowers?

Buy them tomorrow.

¿Adónde llevo a las niñas?

Llévalas a casa de su abuela.

Where do I take the girls?

Take them to their grandmother's house.

¿Quieres que le dé los regalos a Juan?

Sí, dáselos mañana.

Do you want me to give Juan the gifts?

Yes, give them to him tomorrow.

¿A quién se lo entrego?

Entrégueselo a la Profesora Muñoz.

Who do I hand this in to?

Hand it in to Professor Muñoz.

EXERCISE 3.21

Answer the following questions with an affirmative command. Use the form noted in parenthesis.

Example: Pedrito y Claudia quieren ir a la fiesta. ¿Los llevo?
     Sí, llévalos.

1. Andrés y Alejandro están en la estación de tren.
¿Los recojo? (tú)

2. Hay unas blusas de seda que me gustan. ¿Las compro? (Ud.)

3. Tengo dolor de cabeza. ¿Puedo tomar estas aspirinas? (Ud.)

4. La directora me ha pedido este documento. ¿Se lo envío? (tú)

5. Rita necesita cien dólares. ¿Se los presto? (Ud.)

NEGATIVE COMMANDS

In the case of negative commands, the object pronouns (direct, indirect, reflexive) are placed BEFORE the verbs.

The examples have an initial negative command, and then a related affirmative command to contrast the position of the pronouns.

> Nos vamos mañana.
>
> No se vayan todavía. Quédense un poco más.
> *We are leaving tomorrow.*
> *Don't leave yet. Stay a little longer.*
>
> ¿Pongo las cajas aquí?
>
> No, no las pongas aquí. Ponlas junto a la ventana.
> *Do you want me to put the boxes here?*
> *No, don't put them here. Put them next to the window.*
>
> ¿Perdono a Guillermo?
>
> ¡No, no lo perdones! ¡Olvídalo!
> *Do I forgive Guillermo?*
> *No, don't forgive him! Forget about him!*
>
> ¿Le traigo un café ahora?
>
> No, no me lo traiga todavía. Tráigame un vaso de agua.
> *Shall I bring a cup of expresso now?*
> *No, don't bring it (to me) yet. Bring me a glass of water.*

EXERCISE 3.22

Answer the following questions with a negative command.

> Example: Pedro y Claudia quieren venir a la fiesta. ¿Los invito? *No, no los invites.*

1. ¿Recojo a Carmen?

2. ¿Preparo la cena?

3. ¿Compramos los regalos en esta tienda?

4. ¿Sirvo la sopa de pollo?

4

Talking Hypothetically

When we talk about the future we are essentially talking about the hypothetical. Think about it: No one can be one-hundred percent sure of what will happen.

THE FUTURE

To talk about what will definitely happen, or what is within the realm of possibility, use the future indicative.

Example:
Mi hija tendrá que ir a la escuela mañana.

My daughter will have to go to school tomorrow.

Well, unless an unexpected ruling were to come down from the Supreme Court legislating that children did not have to go to school tomorrow, we can consider this a done deal. The probability of the statement being true is so great that it is considered definite, thus the future indicative tense. Remember, the indicative mood is used to state facts and ask questions.

Things get funky when we get into statements like:

Si yo me ganara la lotería, iría a Madrid a estudiar español.

If I were to win the lottery, I would go to Madrid to study Spanish!

That sentence refers to the future, yes, but how likely is this scenario? You decide!

Anyway, back to the future. The Spanish future tense is translated as will + the infinitive.

Example:

Me graduaré en mayo.

I will graduate in May.

Tomaremos unas vacaciones en Europa.

We will vacation in Europe.

Regresarán el año que viene.

They will return next year.

FORMATION

Forming the future with regular verbs is easy. Simply add the following endings to the infinitive form of the verb.

-é	-emos
-ás	-éis
-á	-án

hablar, comer, vivir

	hablar	comer	vivir
yo	hablaré	comeré	viviré
tú	hablarás	comerás	vivirás
él/ella/Ud.	hablará	comerá	vivirá
nosotros	hablaremos	comeremos	viviremos
vosotros	hablaréis	comeréis	viviréis
ellos/ellas/Uds.	hablarán	comerán	vivirán

Note: The last syllable is always accented in the future, except in the *nosotros* form.

EXERCISE 4.1

María talks about her plans for success as an actress. Fill in the blanks with the regular future verbs indicated.

Soy María González y éstos son mis planes. Me graduaré de la universidad este año. Después de tomar un mes de vacaciones, ___1___ (ir) a Nueva York. ___2___ (trabajar) de mesera para ganar suficiente dinero para vivir. Pero de noche, ___3___ (asistir a) clases de baile, canto y actuación. Algún día yo ___4___ (ser) famosa y mi público me ___5___ (aplaudir) y me ___6___ (gritar) "¡Brava! ¡Bravísima!" Mis padres ___7___ (sentirse) muy orgullosos. Los reporteros me ___8___ (preguntar), "¿A qué le debes tu estrellato, tu fama?" Yo ___9___ (sonreír) y les ___10___ (explicar) que mi familia me ha apo-yado y les ___11___ (dar) las gracias públicamente. Ese día, mis sueños ___12___ (realizarse).

EXERCISE 4.2

Emilio went to see an astrologer. Fill in the future tense form of the verb.

1. Emilio, tú _____ la mujer ideal. (encontrar)

2. Uds. _____ en un castillo en España. (casarse)

3. Los invitados a la boda les _____ millones de dólares. (regalar)

4. Los dos _____ por el mundo entero durante la luna de miel. (viajar)

5. Yo te _____ mucho dinero porque soy la mejor astróloga del mundo. (cobrar)

IR + A + INFINITIVE

Spanish speakers tend to use the *ir + a + infinitive* construction more than the future tense in everyday conversation.

La astróloga va a predecir su porvenir.

The astrologer is going to predict his future.

Simply conjugate the verb *ir*, add *a* and then the infinitive.

ir — to go

Singular	Plural
yo voy	nosotros vamos
tú vas	vosotros váis
él/ella/Ud. va	ellos/ellas/Uds. van

Look at the conversation between Emilio and Matilde, his astrologer. Notice the use of the *ir + a +* infinitive construction to discuss the future.

Emilio: Buenos días, Matilde. ¿Cómo será mi vida amorosa?

Matilde: Oh, Emilio. Tú vas a encontrar la mujer ideal y se van a casar en un castillo español. Los invitados a la boda les van a regalar mucho dinero y van a viajar los dos alrededor del mundo.

Emilio: ¡Qué bien! ¡Voy a ser un hombre feliz!

Matilde: Y yo voy a ser una mujer feliz. Tú me vas a pagar trescientos dólares en efectivo.

Translation

Emilio: *Good morning, Matilde. What is my love life going to be like?*

Matilde: *Oh, Emilio. You are going to meet the ideal woman and you will marry in a Spanish castle. Your guests will give you lots of money and the two of you will travel around the world.*

Emilio: *That is great! I will be a happy man!*

Matilde: *I will be a happy woman too. You are going to pay me three hundred dollars in cash.*

EXERCISE 4.3

Read the conversation between José and his son Joaquín. Fill in the appropriate form of the verb using the *ir + a +* infinitive construction.

José: Joaquín, tengo buenas noticias. Si no llueve el sábado, _____1_____(ir) al parque.

Joaquín: ¡Qué bien! Me gusta estar afuera cuando hace buen tiempo.

José: Claro, Joaquín. _____2_____(salir) temprano
y _____3_____(pasar) el día entero juntos.
Elena _____4_____(venir), también. Yo sé que ella
_____5_____(querer) ir con nosotros. A ella
también le gusta ir al parque. Yo __6__ (ponerse)
en contacto con ella mañana por la mañana para
saber si _____7_____(poder) venir.

Joaquín: Mañana _____8_____(ser) un día fantástico!

IRREGULAR VERBS IN THE FUTURE TENSE

There are some irregular stems in the future, of course. You didn't
think you'd be let off that easily, did you? The endings, however,
don't change. Look at the verb *decir*, for example.

decir — to say	
yo	diré
tú	dirás
él/ella/Ud.	dirá
nosotros	diremos
vosotros	diréis
ellos/ellas/Uds.	dirán

While the root is not the infinitive, but rather *dir-*, the endings stay
the same as the regular future tense verbs. Here are some other
verbs that have irregular stems in the future.

There are three groups. Let's look at them.

In the first group, these *-er* verbs drop the *e* to form the future stem.

Infinitive	Future stem	Yo form
caber — to fit	cabr	yo cabré
haber — to have (helping verb)	habr	yo habré
poder — to be able to	podr	yo podré
querer — to want; to desire	querr	yo querré

In the second group, these -er or –ir verbs change the e or i to form the future stem:

Infinitive	Future stem	Yo form
poner — to put	pondr	yo pondré
salir — to go out	saldr	yo saldré
tener — to have	tendr	yo tendré
valer — to be worth	valdr	yo valdré
venir — to come	vendr	yo vendré

There are only two words in the group. These verbs drop both letters.

Infinitive	Future stem	Yo form
hacer — to do	har	yo haré
decir — to say	dir	yo diré

EXERCISE 4.4

This time, fill in appropriate future form of the indicated verb.

José: Joaquín, tengo buenas noticias. Si no llueve el sábado, _____1_____(ir) al parque.

Joaquín: !Qué bien! Me gusta estar afuera cuando hace buen tiempo.

José: Claro, Joaquín. _____2_____(salir) temprano y _____3_____(pasar) el día entero juntos. Elena _____4_____(venir), también. Yo sé que ella _____5_____ (querer) ir con nosotros. A ella también le gusta ir al parque. Yo __6__(ponerse) en contacto con ella mañana por la mañana para saber si _____7_____(poder) venir.

Joaquín: ¡Mañana _____8_____(ser) un día fantástico!

THE FUTURE OF *HAY*

The future of *hay* (there is, there are) is also irregular. Since it is an impersonal verb, it exists only in the singular: *habrá*.

Habrá una persona importante en tu vida.

There will be an important person in your life.

Habrá cientos de invitados en tu boda.

There will be hundreds of guests at your wedding.

EXERCISE 4.5

Give the future of *hay* in the following sentences.

1. _____ más de tres mil reporteros en presencia.

2. ¿Cuántas obras _____ en la exposición este año?

3. _____ un personaje principal en el segundo acto de la obra.

4. No quedan panecillos aquí. ¿_____ en casa de Luisa?

5. ¿_____ algún trato entre los dos países acerca de este asunto?

THE PLOT THICKENS

Now let's start adding layers. Let's see what happens when you state conditions and how they might affect the future.

Look at the following excerpts from a conversation José and María are having about their 22-year-old son who is studying in Buenos Aires. They are speculating about what he might be doing right now, given different conditions.

Si hace buen tiempo, está en el parque.

If the weather is good, he is in the park.

El estudia en la biblioteca si tiene mucha tarea que hacer.

He is studying in the library if he has a lot of homework to do.

Si tiene el dinero, invita a Elena a cenar el sábado.

If he has the money, he will treat Elena to dinner on Saturday.

In this construction, both the main and dependent clauses are in the present indicative tense. The structure *si* is used to express a conclusion about the present.

Si Juan aprende bien el español tiene más posibilidades de conseguir un puesto en la sucursal del D.F.

If Juan learns Spanish well, he will have a better chance of landing a position at the Mexico City branch.

To state resulting actions, or events, should certain conditions be met, use this construction:

1. Si (if) + present indicative verb + verb in the present

   Si los López no llegan a tiempo, tenemos que irnos sin ellos.

   If the Lopez family does not arrive on time, we have to leave without them.

2. Si (if) + present indicative verb + verb in the future

   Si los López no llegan a tiempo, tendremos que irnos sin ellos.

   If the Lopez family does not arrive on time, we will have to leave without them.

NOTE: The order of the clauses does not affect the meaning.

Si los López no llegan a tiempo, tenemos que irnos sin ellos is exactly the same as saying *tenemos que irnos sin los López si no llegan a tiempo.*

Si los López no llegan a tiempo, tendremos que irnos sin ellos is exactly the same as saying *tendremos que irnos sin los López si no llegan a tiempo.*

EXERCISE 4.6

What will you do under the following conditions?

Examples:

Si tienes ganas de comer paella, ¿qué haces?

If you feel like eating paella, what do you do?

Si tengo ganas de comer paella, voy a un restaurante español.

If I feel like eating paella, I will go to a Spanish restaurant.

1. Si tienes mucho dinero, ¿qué te compras?

2. Si su coche se le descompone en la carretera, ¿qué hará?

3. Si aparece una llamada en su cuenta telefónica que Ud. no reconoce, ¿qué hace?

4. ¿Cómo reacciona si recibe una carta de amor anónima?

The future tense is used to express a conclusion made about the future.

Ganará buena plata si consigue el puesto.
He will make good money if he gets the job.

Si no tiene que trabajar este fin de semana, irá a Brasil con Elena.
If he doesn't have to work this weekend, he will go to the Brasil with Elena.

Main clause: *Irá a Brasil con Elena* can stand alone grammatically. It's a full sentence, a complete idea.

Dependent clause: *Si no tiene que trabajar este fin de semana* is not a full sentence. This clause "depends" on the main clause for its meaning to become a complete idea, so it's the dependent clause.

The order of the clauses does not affect the meaning of the structure.

Si no tiene que trabajar este fin de semana, irá a Brasil con Elena is exactly the same as saying *Irá a Brasil con Elena si no tiene que trabajar este fin de semana.*

EXERCISE 4.7

Matching columns. Match each *si* or condition clause to the logical dependent clause.

1. Si me gano la lotería,

2. Si el banco me hace el préstamo (loan),

3. Si la profesora me pide la tarea,

4. Si hace mal tiempo mañana,

5. Si me piden la identificación en la discoteca,

A más nunca trabajaré.

B le diré que mi perro se la comió.

C cancelarán las clases.

D me compraré el coche.

E tendremos que ir a otro sitio a bailar.

EXERCISE 4.8

Now finish the following statements. Possible answers are given in the answer key.

1. Si en EEUU eligen a una mujer presidente, las feministas...

2. Si algún día es posible vivir en la luna, mis amigos y yo...

3. Si los Yankees ganan la Series Mundial, los neoyorquinos...

4. Si mis amigos me preparan una fiesta sorpresa para mi próximo cumpleaños, yo...

5. Si computadora no funciona mañana, mi...

TALKING ABOUT WHAT MIGHT, COULD, OR WOULD HAPPEN

In the constructions above we have only used the future and/or combinations of the present and future indicative. But there is another way to talk about what is possible, that is, what might, could, or would happen. Spanish, like English, uses the *conditional* tense:

1. to talk about an action that one could do if something else were possible.

    Si tuviera el dinero, me compraría un Mercedes Benz.
    If I had the money, I would buy myself a Mercedes Benz.

2. to express a desire. This is called the conditional of courtesy.

    Me gustaría hablar más contigo. (Si me dejaras.)
    I would like to talk to you some more. (If you are willing to let me.)

3. when quoting someone indirectly.

    Jose dijo que María llegaría antes de las diez.
    José said María would arrive before ten.

    José me explicó que el vuelo se restrasaría un por de horas.

José told me that the flight would be delayed by a couple of hours.

4. to speculate about something in the past.

¿Me pregunto quién sería?
I wonder who that was.

5. to discuss a probable condition in the past.

Estaría lloviendo cuando despegó el avión.
It was probably raining when the plane took off.

FORMATION

To form the conditional, add the following endings to the infinitive form of the verb. The stem for the conditional is the same as the stem for the future.

	hablar	**comer**	**ir**
yo	hablaría	comería	iría
tú	hablarías	comerías	irías
él/ella/Ud.	hablaría	comería	iría
nosotros	hablaríamos	comeríamos	iríamos
vosotros	hablaríais	comeríais	iríais
ellos/ellas/Uds.	hablarían	comerían	irían

THINGS TO REMEMBER

1. Both the future and the conditional have the same stem, so be careful not to mix them up.

Future:

Estudiaremos matemáticas mañana.
We will study math tomorrow.

Conditional:

Estudiaríamos matemáticas también si tuviéramos más tiempo.
We would study math as well if we had more time.

2. The first person and third person singular are identical in the conditional.

> Yo hablaría portugués si fuera brasileña.
> *I would speak Portuguese if I were Brazilian.*

> Ella hablaría portugués si fuera brasileña.
> *She would speak Portuguese if she were Brazilian.*

The order of the clauses do not affect the meaning of these conditional sentences.

> Si fuera brasileña, hablaría portugués. = Hablaría portugués si fuera brasileña.

> *If she were Brazilian, she would speak Portuguese. = She would speak Portuguese if she were Brazilian.*

EXERCISE 4.9

Tell what would or wouldn't happen under the following conditions.

Example:

> Si/Oprah/lograr/presidencia/ser/primer/mujer/presidente

> Si Oprah lograra la presidencia, sería la primera mujer presidente.

1. Si/el presidente/legalizar/consumo/marihuana/conservadores/oponerse a la medida.

2. Si/Ricky Martin/no/bailar/bien/no/ser/tan/popular

3. Si/mi computadora/ser/más rápida/yo/terminar/mí trabajo/antes.

4. Si/el racismo/no existir/mundo/ser/maravilloso.

5. Si/se/inventar/coches eléctricos/aire/estar/más limpio.

One of the most important uses of the conditional tense is to express what would or would not happen if something else were (or were not) to happen.

Example:

> What would happen in the following hypothetical situations?
> *If I were to win the lottery?*

I would quit my job and travel the world.

If I were to lose my job?

I would have to get another one.

This type of sentence is called contrary-to-fact condition. What is the likelihood of me winning the lottery? Nil! The *si* clause states something that is not a fact nor is likely to become a fact in the future. In contrary-to-fact conditions, Spanish speakers use the imperfect subjunctive in the *si* clause. For example, *Si ganara la lotería... Si ferdiera mi trabajo...,* and the conditional in the result clause, which states what would be the outcome should that contrary-to-fact statement become true. *Yo dejaría mi puesto y viajaría alrededor del mundo.*

Note that the order of the clauses is not important; the following sentences mean the same thing:

> *Si fuera Bill Gates, donaría millones de dólares a los pobres* is exactly the same as saying *Donaría millones de dólares a los pobres si fuera Bill Gates.*

> *If I were Bill Gates, I would donate millions of dollars to the poor* is exactly the same as saying *I would donate millions of dollars to the poor if I were Bill Gates.*

EXERCISE 4.10

What would one do? Write contrary to fact statements using the following clues. Use the subject pronoun indicated.

Examples:

yo/estar resfriado/tomar sopa de pollo.

Si yo estuviera resfriado, tomaría sopa de pollo.

ellos/ir/a Madrid/comer tapas.

Si ellos fueran a Madrid, comerían tapas.

1. Él/hablar/español/trabajar/México.

2. Nosotros/ser/haitianos/hablar/francés.

3. Tú/tomarse/cerveza/emborracharse/en seguida.

4. Ella/pensar/en su carrera/no/dejar/su trabajo.

5. Los BMW/no costar/tanto/comprar/uno/mi amor.

Last but not least is a structure that is used to refer to actions, events, or situations that are not part of reality: *como si.*

> Ella me mira como si yo estuviera loco.
>
> *She looks at me as if I were crazy.*

> Ella actuaba como si no hubiera pasado nada.
>
> *She would act as if nothing had happened.*

In the first example, the statement refers to the present and the *como si* clause requires its verbs to be in the imperfect subjunctive.

In the second sentence, the action expressed in the *como si* clause took place before the verb in the dependent clause; that's why it is in the past perfect subjunctive.

EXERCISE 4.11

Match each main clause to the logical dependent clause.

1. Mis amigos me miran

2. ¿Quién baila

3. Las admiradores de Ricky Martin le gritan

4. La policía me habla

5. ¿Por qué me hablas

A como si él fuera un dios.

B como si yo fuera el culpable.

C como si tuviera una cucaracha en los pantalones?

D como si yo estuviera loca.

E como si yo no te entendiera?

Answer Key for Chapter Exercises

CHAPTER 1

Exercise 1.2

1. Sí, Ricky Martin habla bien el español.
2. Sí, Madona tiene una hija que se llama Lourdes.
3. No, Brad Pitt no tiene pelo negro.
4. Sí, Michael Jordan juega bien al baloncesto.

Exercise 1.3

1. A
2. E
3. C
4. D
5. G
6. B
7. F

Exercise. 1.4

1. ¿Cómo
2. ¿Cómo
3. ¿Dónde
4. ¿Cuál
5. ¿Cuántos
6. ¿Cuándo
7. ¿Cuál?
8. ¿Por qué
9. ¿Cuánto

Exercise. 1.5

1. ¿Quiénes
2. ¿Cuándo
3. ¿Adónde
4. ¿De dónde
5. ¿Cuánto
6. ¿Dónde

Exercise 1.6

la=feminine el=masculine
1. la biblioteca
2. la casa
3. la costumbre
4. la ciudad
5. el dolor
6. la especie
7. el guacamole
8. la inspiración
9. el interés
10. el jardín
11. la libertad
12. el libro
13. el Japón
14. el papel
15. el parque

Exercise 1.7

los=masculine las=feminine
1. las discotecas
2. las especies
3. la frustración
4. los hijos
5. los horrores
6. el japonés
7. la japonesa
8. las libertades
9. las mesas
10. la muchedumbre
11. el tamal
12. el tapiz
13. el terror

Exercise. 1.8

Only 2, 4 and 5 need correction.
2. al novio
4. del Ecuador
5. del Caribe

Exercise 1.9
1. los libros
2. unas mesas
3. las computadoras
4. unos mesones
5. unos pollos
6. unas paredes
7. los españoles
8. las españolas
9. unos jueces
10. los lápices
11. unos coches
12. unos tapices

Exercise 1.11
1. Se despierta a las 6:30 de la mañana.
2. Se levanta a las 7 de la mañana.
3. Ella se baña rápidamente.
4. Se seca el cuerpo con una toalla.
5. Se pone la ropa.
6. Se desayuna café con leche y pan tostado.
7. Se pone un poco de maquillaje en la cara.
8. Se pone su perfume preferido.
9. Se prepara una cena saludable.
10. Se acuesta a las 10 de la noche.

Exercise 1.10
1. José juega bien al baloncesto.
2. Los vecinos me despiertan a las 6:00 de la mañana.
3. A veces los alumnos no entienden la lección.
4. En mi casa, nosotros almorzamos a las 2:30 de la tarde.
5. ¿Cuánto cuesta el café?
6. Yo no recuerdo bien la dirección.
7. ¿A qué hora vuelven tus padres?
8. Si yo no duermo suficientemente, no puedo trabajar mañana.
9. La dependiente envuelve el regalo.
10. José consigue buenos precios en K-Mart.

Exercise 1.12

1. Se vende una casa grande
2. Se compran camaras de segunda mano.
3. Se busca una profesora de español.
4. Se alquila una habitación en un apartamento céntrico
5. Se traducen documentos oficiales.

Exercise 1.13

1. nada
2. nadie
3. nunca
4. ninguna
5. ninguno

Exercise 1.14

1. está jugando
2. está arañando
3. está hablando
4. se están subiendo/están subiéndose
5. están cantando

Exercise 1.15

1. están durmiendo
2. está sirviendo
3. estás leyendo
4. están riendose
5. está diciendo

Exercise 1.16

1. introvertida
2. organizado
3. simpático
4. atlético
5. reservada

Exercise 1.17

1. C
2. D
3. A
4. B

Exercise 1.18

1. polaco
2. italiana
3. francesa
4. español
5. puertorriqueño
6. puertorriqueños
7. cubano
8. cubana

Exercise 1.19

1. José es cruel; abusa de los animales péquenos, como los gatitos.
2. José es extrovertido; hace los papales principales en las obras teatrales de la escuela.
3. José es franco; dice exactamente lo que piensa.
4. José es intelectual; habla mucho de sus idea políticas y filosóficas.
5. José es inteligente; entiende avanzados conceptos matemáticos.
6. José es reservado; no habla mucho de su vida privada.
7. José es sentimental; llora mucho cuando ve películas románticas.
8. José es tímido; se le pone roja la cara cuando le hablan.

Exercise 1.20

1. explanation
2. possibly
3. biology
4. fraternity
5. participate

Exercise 1.21

1. mi
2. tu
3. su
4. nuestros
5. vuestras
6. sus

Exercise 1.22

1. D
2. A
3. B
4. C
5. F
6. E

Exercise .1.23

1. D
2. E
3. A
4. B
5. C
6. F

Exercise 1.24

1. tengo prisa o estoy apurado
2. tenemos hambre
3. tengo frío
4. tienen sed
5. tengo hambre
6. está nerviosa
7. tienen miedo
8. está de mal humor
9. está enojada

Exercise 1.25

1. rico
2. extrovertidos
3. mejor
4. alta
5. mayor

Exercise. 1.26

1. canciones
2. discos
3. inglés
4. pobres

Exercise 1.27

1. C
2. F
3. A
4. B
5. E
6. D

CHAPTER 2

Exercise 2.1

1. acaban
2. acaba
3. acabo
4. acaban
5. acabamos

Exercise 2.2

1. hablé
2. inmigraron
3. comieron
4. bebió
5. participó

Exercise 2.3

1. Sí, salí con ellos anoche.
   No, no salí ...
2. Sí, estudié en la biblioteca.
   No, no estudié...
3. Sí, trabajé muchas horas anoche.
   No, no trabajé...
4. Sí, comí un dulce ayer.
   No, no comí ninguno.
5. Sí, lo llamé.
   No, no lo llamé.

Exercise 2.4

1. anduvieron
2. estuvieron
3. puso
4. conduje
5. dije

Exercise 2.5

1. ser
2. ser
3. ir
4. ir
5. ser

Exercise 2.6

1. empecé
2. utilizaron
3. me encargué
4. cargué
5. saqué

Exercise 2.7

1. pensó
2. jugaron
3. leímos
4. di
5. oyeron

Exercise 2.8

1. mintió
2. prefirieron
3. sirví
4. nos divertimos
5. advirtieron

Exercise 2.9

1. Abuela, ¿cuál **era** su juego preferido de niña?
2. Yo **jugaba** a la bebeleche con mis hermanas.
3. ¿**Tenía** Ud. tareas en la casa?
4. Sí, María. Yo **ayudaba** a mi madre en la cocina. Yo **preparaba** la cena para todo el mundo cuando ella **tenía** que trabajar fuera de la casa.
5. La vida en el campo **era** dura, pero divertida también?

Exercise 2.10

1. iba
2. dieron
3. llegaron
4. estudiaron
5. estaban

Exercise 2.11

Era el domingo por la noche. *Eran* las tres de la mañana. *Hacía* mucho calor en la casa de la Sra. Miranda. Todas las ventanas *estaban* abiertas y la Sra. Miranda *dormía* profundamente en su cuarto. A las tres en punto, un joven *pasó* por el frente de la casa. *Tenía* 21 años. *Era* alto, fuerte y *llevaba* bigotes. El *entró* por la ventana de la sala y se *sentó* en el sofá. *Admiró* las pinturas en la pared y los muebles elegantes. Después de unos minutos *fue* a la cocina, *abrió* el refrigerador y *vio* que *había* mucha comida y un fino vino italiano. Se *preparó* un sándwich de pollo y se *sirvió* un vaso de vino tinto. Se *sentó* en la mesa del comedor, *comió* y *bebió* tranquilamente. Mientras *comía, pensó* que la señora Miranda *era* muy buena cocinera. Se *comió* todo el sándwich y se *tomó* la botella entera de vino. Se *emborrachó* tanto que *cayó* al piso y el ruido *despertó* a la Sra. Miranda. Asustada, *bajó* las escaleras con su pistola en las manos y *descubrió* un hombre en la cocina. Al *acercarse* y mirarle la cara, se *dio* cuenta de que *era* José, su jardinero que dormía en el piso. De repente *sintió* una brisa fuerte, y se *dio* cuenta de que *estaban* abiertas las ventanas. *Fue* a cerrarlas, *sonrió*, y *regresó* a su cama.

Exercise 2.12

1. estaba jugando
2. estaba llorando
3. estábamos tomando
4. estaban haciendo
5. estaban preparando

Exercise 2.13

1. han logrado
2. ha tenido
3. han llegado
1. he cambiado
2. hemos decidido

Exercise 2.14

1. ¿Has manejado un Mercedes-Benz?
   Sí, he manejado un Mercedes-Benz.
   No, nunca he manejado un Mercedes-Benz.
2. ¿Has bailado la cha-cha-chá?
   Sí, he bailado la cha-cha-chá.
   No, nunca he bailado el cha-cha-chá.
3. ¿Has asistido a clases de matemáticas?
   Sí, he asistido a clases de matemáticas.
   No, nunca he asistido a clases de matemáticas.
4. ¿Has hecho fiestas en tu casa?
   Sí, he hecho fiestas en tu casa.
   No, nunca he hecho fiestas en tu casa.
5. ¿Has estado en Buenos Aires?
   Sí, he estado en Buenos Aires.
   No, nunca he estado en Buenos Aires.

Exercise 2.15

1. Mi madre nunca había hablado inglés.
2. Mi padre ya había estudiado medecina.
3. Nosotors nunca habíamos visto la nieve
4. Mis tías nunca habían manejado un auto.
5. Yo nunca había visto Disneyland.

Exercise 2.16

1. Cuando decidiste ir al cine, la película ya había empezado.
2. Cuando encendiste el televisor, tu programa preferido ya había terminado.
3. Cuando fuiste a la tienda para comprar un nuevo programa para la computadora, ya se había agotado.
4. Cuando buscaste a un amigo en un "Chat Room", é ya se había desconectado de la Red.
5. Cuando sacaste la tarjeta de crédito para pagar, ya había pasado su fecha de expiración.

CHAPTER 3
Exercise 3.1

1. vivan
2. coman
3. baile
4. hablen
5. viajemos

Exercise 3.2

1. pongan
2. recoja
3. conduzca
4. vengan
5. construyas

Exercise 3.3

1. se eduquen
2. se equivoquen
3. critique
4. busquen
5. me acerque

Exercise 3.4

1. despegue
2. colonicen
3. calce
4. peguen
5. organice

Exercise 3.5

1. despierten
2. se sientan
3. me confiese
4. nieguen
5. atraviese

Exercise 3.6

1. se diviertan
2. se sientan
3. quiera
4. quieran
5. os divirtáis

Exercise 3.7

1. almuercen
2. se prueben
3. vuele
4. demuestren
5. encuentre

Exercise 3.8

1. puedan
2. muevan
3. llueva
4. envuelvan
5. devuelva

Exercise 3.9

José quiere que María **sea** su esposa, pero ella no lo quiere. Él desea que ella **esté** a su lado para siempre y le **dé** muchos hijos. María le ha dicho que no, pero él insiste en que ella **vaya** con él hasta el fin del mundo. Y aunque ella le diga que no iría ni hasta la esquina con él, él insiste en necesario que ella **sepa** cuánto la quiere para que cambie de idea. Temo que José padezca del terrible síndrome de Don Quijote.

Exercise 3.10

Answers will vary.

1. Es escandaloso que las mujeres **ganen** menos que los hombres.
2. Es ridículo que los estadounidenses **sean** fanáticos del fútbol americano.
3. Es bueno que la Internet **ofrezca** una enorme cantidad de información.
4. Es una lástima que el número de divorcios **aumente** cada año.

Exercise 3.11

1. El médico le recomienda al paciente haga ejercicios.
2. El psicólogo le sugiere al cliente que hable acerca de su niñez traumática.
3. La profesora quiere que los estudiantes escriban tres párrafos sobre el tema.
4. La madre prefiere que su hija se ponga el vestido rosado.
5. El chófer necesita que el pasajero cierre la ventanilla del carro.

Exercise 3.12

1. estén
2. podamos
3. tengas
4. quiera
5. sepan

Exercise 3.13

1. hayan ganado
2. haya venido
3. se hayan perdido
4. hayan decidido
5. hayas traído

Exercise 3.14

Preterite
1. anduvieron
2. dieron
3. durmieron
4. hicieron
5. fueron
6. leyeron
7. pudieron
8. quisieron
9. fueron
10. trajeron

Imperfect subjunctive
1. anduviera
2. diera
3. durmiera
4. hiciera
5. fuera
6. leyera
7. pudiera
8. quisiera
9. fuera
10. trajera

Exercise 3.15

1. disfrutara
2. preparara
3. funcionara
4. vinieran
5. se ocupara

Exercise 3.16

1. bajara
2. fuera
3. prestara
4. se casara
5. tuviera

Exercise 3.17

1. Los aficionados lamentaron que los Mets no hubieran ganado la Serie Mundial.
2. Me alegré de que mi hermano hubiera conocido a Chayanne.
3. Miguel sintió que el protagonista hubiera muerto.
4. Dudaba de que mi hijo hubiera cometido un delito.

Exercise 3.18

1. gradúe
2. llegue
3. tome
4. logre
5. tenga
6. sea

Exercise 3.19

Yo form of the present indicative	Ud. command	Uds. command
1. como	1. coma	1. coman
2. estudio	2. estudie	2. estudien
3. camino	3. camine	3. caminen
4. decido	4. decida	4. decidan
5. cambio	5. cambie	5. cambien

Exercise 3.20

1. Préstale
2. Haz
3. Practica
4. Pon
5. Lava

Exercise 3.21

1. Sí, recójelos.
2. Sí, cómprelas.
3. Sí, tómeselas.
4. Sí, envíaselo.
5. Sí, présteselos.

Exercise 3.22

1) No, no la recojas.
2) No, no la prepares.
3) No, no los compres.
4) No, no la sirves.

CHAPTER 4
Exercise 4.1

1. iré
2. trabajaré
3. asistiré a
4. seré
5. aplaudirá
6. gritará
7. se sentirán
8. preguntarán
9. sonreiré
10. explicaré
11. daré
12. se realizarán

Exercise 4.2

1. encontrarás
2. se casarán
3. regalarán
4. viajarán
5. cobraré

Exercise 4.3

1. vamos a ir
2. vamos a salir
3. vamos a pasar
4. va a venir
5. va a querer
6. me voy a poner
7. va a poder
8. va a ser

Exercise 4.4

1. iremos
2. saldremos
3. pasaremos
4. vendrá
5. querrá
6. me pondré
7. podrá
8. será

Exercise 4.5

1. Habrá
2. habrá
3. Habrá
4. habrá
5. Habrá

Exercise 4.6

(Answers will vary.)

1. Si tengo mucho dinero, compro suéteres y zapatos caros.
2. Llamaré a AAA si mi coche se me descompone en la carretera.
3. Si aparece una llamada en mi cuenta telefónica que no reconozco, hablo con mis compañeros de cuarto.
4. Me pongo muy contento si recibo una carta de amor anónima.

Exercise 4.7

1. A
2. D
3. B
4. C
5. E

Exercise 4.8

Answers will vary.

1. Si los EEUU eligen a una mujer presidente, las feministas estarán muy contentas.
2. Si algún día es posible vivir en la luna, mis amigos y yo seremos los primeros en ir para allá.
3. Si los Yankees ganan la Serie Mundial, los neoyorquinos se volverán locos de alegría.
4. Si mis amigos me preparan una fiesta sorpresa para mi próximo cumpleaños, yo me pondré rojo de bochorno.
5. Si mi computadora no funciona mañana, no podré terminar este trabajo de investigación.

Exercise 4.9

1. Si el presidente legalizara el consumo de marihuana, los conservadores se opondrían a la medida.
2. Si Ricky Martin no bailara tan bien, no sería tan popular.
3. Si mi computadora fuera más rápida, yo terminaría mi trabajo antes.
4. Si el racismo no existiera, el mundo sería maravilloso.
5. Si se inventaran coches eléctricos, el aire estaría más limpio.

Exercise 4.10

1. Si él hablara español, trabajaría en México.
2. Si nosotros fuéramos haitianos, hablaríamos francés.
3. Si tú te tomaras una cerveza, te emborracharías en seguida.
4. Si ella pensara en su carrera, no dejaría su trabajo.
5. Si los BMW no costaran tanto, te compraría uno, mi amor.

Exercise 4.11

1. D
2. C
3. A
4. B
5. E

Sample Test I

PART 1

Answer all questions in Part 1 according to the directions for *a* and *b*. [30]

Listening Comprehension passages begin on page 181.

(a) Directions (1–9): For each question, you will hear some background information in English *once*. Then you will hear a passage in Spanish *twice* and a question in English *once*. After you have heard the question, the teacher will pause while you read the question and the four suggested answers on your test. Choose the best suggested answer and write its *number* in the space provided on your answer sheet. Base your answer *on the content of the passage, only*. [18]

---

1 As a child, what did this celebrity always want to do?

   1 become an artist
   2 visit other countries
   3 perform in the theater
   4 learn several languages

2 What information does this announcement give to tourists?

   1 There will be a short delay due to problems at Customs.
   2 Food and beverages will be served during the flight.
   3 Travelers bringing produce into the United States will be fined.
   4 Passengers traveling with young children will board first.

3 Why is a new price being advertised?

   1 as a result of an increase in mailing costs
   2 as a result of a delay in the production schedule
   3 as a result of a temporary labor problem
   4 as a result of a special supplement

4 What message did Alicia leave on the answering machine?

   1 She forgot to buy the watch.
   2 The jeweler did not have the gift ready.
   3 Her father borrowed her car for the day.
   4 She was unable to do the favor you wanted.

5 Where did this traveler spend most of her time?

   1 relaxing on the beach in Belize
   2 visiting ruins from an ancient civilization
   3 shopping in a large historical city
   4 visiting historical museums in Belize

6 How did Angélica Rivera achieve international fame?

   1 She was a model with several foreign agencies.
   2 Her soap opera was televised in other countries.
   3 She was a conductor of a Mexican orchestra.
   4 her appearance in Mexican commercials made her popular.

7 What does this message concern?

   1 disconnecting telephone service
   2 a new answering machine
   3 additional telephone numbers
   4 changes in telephone rates

8 How would visitors to this small village in Spain participate in its festival?

   1 by throwing ripe tomatoes
   2 by marching in a parade
   3 by tasting a variety of regional dishes
   4 by dancing in the streets

9 What new type of product is being made available to consumers?

   1 vegetables that are grown in water rather than soil
   2 vitamins that can replace many foods
   3 products that are natural and healthy
   4 foods that are easy to prepare

Directions (10–15): For each question, you will hear some background information in English *once*. Then you will hear a passage in Spanish *twice* and a question in Spanish *once*. After you have heard the question, the teacher will pause while you read the question and the four suggested answers on your test. Choose the best suggested answer and write its *number* in the space provided on your answer sheet. Base your answer *on the content of the passage, only*. [12]

10 ¿De qué trata este anuncio?

  1 el precio de billetes para un juego de béisbol profesional

  2 la falta de respeto de los aficionados

  3 la fabricación de bates de aluminio

  4 el aumento en popularidad de un artículo de ropa de béisbol

11 ¿Cómo se escapa tu amiga de su rutina en el trabajo?

  1 Habla por teléfono con su novio.

  2 Lee su revista favorita.

  3 Contesta su correo personal.

  4 Escucha su música predilecta.

12 ¿Qué beneficio ofrece el sistema Clarión?

  1 Mejora su habilidad como conductor.

  2 Disminuye el número de accidentes.

  3 Hace los viajes menos aburridos.

  4 Reduce la contaminación del ambiente.

13 ¿Por qué no pudo disfrutar la película Geraldo?
   1 porque no podía ver la película
   2 porque no se sentó con sus amigos
   3 porque no era violenta
   4 porque no podía

14 ¿Cuál es una ventaja de este producto?
   1 que alivia el dolor dental al rellenar las caries
   2 que blanquea los dientes sin sustancias químicas
      fuertes
   3 que reduce el mal aliento
   4 que elimina la necesidad de cepillarse los dientes

15 ¿Qué problema tienen Graciela y Rosa?
   1 Dejaron el dinero en casa
   2 Se perdieron en la ciudad.
   3 Llegaron temprano al restaurante.
   4 Tomaron el autobús equivocado.

PART 2

Answer all questions in Part 2 according to the directions for *a*, *b*, and *c*. [30]

(*a*) *Directions* (16–20): After the following passage, there are five questions or incomplete statements. For *each*, choose the word or expression that best answers the question or completes the statement *according to the meaning of the passage*, and write its *number* in the space provided on your answer sheet. [10]

Miguel de Cervantes Saavedra

Me llamo Miguel de Cervantes Saavedra. Mis padres eran nobles pero muy pobres. Mi vida está llena de aventuras de todas clases. Yo creo que nací en Alcalá de Henares en 1547, pero nadie puede a segurarlo. Estudié en la Universidad de Alcalá y en la de Salamanca.

Recuerdo que cuando era niño me gustaba mucho leer. Siempre estaba leyendo. Cuando iba por la calle recogiá los papeles de la calle para leerlos.

A los veintiún años me marché de España para probar mi fortuna. Trabajé al servicio del Cardenal Aquaviva cuando llegué a Roma. Italia me gustó mucho y allí pude leer muchos libros de los escritores clásicos italianos. Pero yo no habiá nacido para ser criado y dos años después me enlisté como soldado en el ejército, y me fui a pelear contra los piratas turcos.

Nuestro jefe era Don Juan de Austria, un príncipe valiente, que era hijo de Carlos V. Peleamos contra los piratas en las ciudades de Corfú, Túnez y Navarino. En 1571 luchamos en el Golfo de Lepanto contra los turcos. En esta batalla yo fui herido en el pecho y en la mano. Perdí el uso de la mano izquierda y por eso me llaman el Manco de Lepanto. Estoy orgulloso de ese apodo.

Pero con una sola mano no podía pelear. Entonces decidí volver a Italia donde pasé el tiempo necesario para curarme y aprender el italiano.

Muchos años después volví a España. ¡Qué triste! Mi padre había muerto, y mi familia estaba en la pobreza. En este punto de mi vida decidí cambiar de carrera. Yo dejé de ser soldado y empecé a escribir. Desde niño siempre tuve interés en la literatura y en escribir.

Estaba yo entonces enamorado de Catalina Salazar y Palacios. Me casé con ella, y ella fue la inspiración para mi primera obra, titulada *La Galatea*. Pero esta novela no tuvo éxito. Entonces dicidí escribir para el teatro y por cuatro años escribía muchas obras breves y unas treinta comedias. De las numerosas obras que yo escribí solamente la *Numancia* y los *Tratos de Argel* tuvieron éxito. Confieso que me dejó muy triste que solamente dos de mis obras tuvieron éxito. Decidí buscar otro trabajo. Encontré un empleo de administración en Sevilla. Pero aún allí me persiguió la mala fortuna. Por hacer un error financiero con el dinero de la compañía me pusieron en la cárcel.

¡Qué días más tristes pasé en la cárcel! Pero, allí empecé a escribir mi primera novela, *El ingenioso hidalgo don Quijote de La Mancha*, también conocido como *Don Quijote*. Por fin lo terminé. Se publicó. Fue un éxito. En un año se publicaron dos ediciones que fueron traducidas a varios idiomas.

Continué escribiendo. Publiqué una colección de *Novelas Ejemplares*; éstas son cuentos cortos sobre costumbres españolas de esta época. También escribí la segunda parte de *Don Quijote*. Muchos críticos creen que la segunda parte de *Don Quijote* es mejor que la primera parte. Lú última obra que escribí fue *Los Trabajos de Persiles y Segismunda*.

Es verdad que mi vida fue muy difícil, pero mis dificultades me hicieron filósofo. Mis aventuras fueron la materia que les dio vida a mis narraciones. Mis viajes me dieron nuevas ideas y material que puedo usar por muchos años. ¡Estoy orgulloso de haber escrito el libro divertido, *Don Quijote*, y de que me llamen *el Manco de Lepanto*!

16 ¿Cuáles son algunos de los trabajos de Miguel de Cervantes?

    1 músico y vendedor
    2 soldado y escritor
    3 carpintero y profesor
    4 biblitecario y médico

17 ¿Qué otro nombre tiene Miguel de Cervantes Saavedra?

    1 Catalina Salazar y Palacios
    2 Don Juan de Austria
    3 Manco de Lepanto
    4 Carlos V

18 ¿Con quién contrae matrimonio Miguel de Cervantes?

1 doña Juana
2 Catalina Salazar y Palacios
3 una mujer italiana
4 una estudiante de la Universidad de Salamanca

19 ¿Dónde comenzó a escribir *Don Quijote*?

1 en la cárcel
2 en la universidad
3 en im teatro
4 en una biblioteca italiana

20 ¿Cuál es el resultado de sus dificultades?

1 Decide abandonar sus sueños.
2 Se casa varias veces cuando era joven.
3 Nunca puede viajar al extranjero.
4 Tiene mucha información para seguir escribiendo.

(b) Directions (21–25): Below each of the following selections, there is either a question or an incomplete statement. For *each*, choose the word or expression that best answers the question or completes the statement *according to the meaning of the selection*, and write its *number* in the space provided on your answer sheet.   [10]

Ahora siempre hay algo bueno en la TV. Gracias a Inglés Sin Barreras, el curso de inglés americano con explicaciones en español.

Nuestros video-cassettes hacen su aprendizaje tan fácil como ver su programa favorito de TV.

Nuestros audio-cassettes mejoran su inglés en su automóvil, en su hogar, o en el trabajo.

Nuestros libros ilustrados le permiten aprender a leer, escribir y practicar lo aprendido.

Lo mejor de todo es que aprenderá inglés en forma natural, mirando, escuchando y repitiendo, tal como aprendió español cuando niño, con la misma escritura, pronunciación y acentos usados en EE.UU.

Su videocasetera se habrá convertido en su mejor maestro.

Empiece a aprender inglés ahora mismo. Llámenos hoy mismo al teléfono **1-800-473-1111**.

---

21 This advertisement provides information about

    1 a way to learn English

    2 a course in television repair

    3 the benefits of using videos in the classroom

    4 a collection of cassettes of popular music

¡Alerta!

Según la División de Agencias de Modelaje nada como una agencia reconocida para descubrir el talento de su niño modelo. Las siguientes son algunas precauciones que debe tomar antes de acudir a una agencia de modelaje:

• Asegúrese de que la agencia tenga licencia del estado.
• Conozca cuanto sea posible sobre la industria del modelaje.
• Esté alerta ante agencias que tratan de presionarla para que invierta dinero en ofertas de fotografía para el portafolio de su niño
• Revise el portafolio de la agencia.
• Solicite una lista de clientes satisfechos. Llámelos y pídales su opinión.
• Desconfíe de los anuncios en la prensa que solicitan modelos infantiles.

22 What advice does this notice give?

1 Children should be dressed in practical clothing.
2 Children should be encouraged to develop artistic talents.
3 A legal contract should be understood before it is signed.
4 The credentials of modeling agencies should be investigated.

Nuevas tarifas de la Edición Internacional de EL PAÍS

A partir de este número, y en coincidencia con el inicio del año 1996, la Edición Internacional de EL PAÍS va a aumentar sus tarifas generales, tanto de suscripción como del precio de portada. Dichas tarifas no habían sufrido variación alguna desde enero de 1991, salvo un pequeño ajuste introducido en abril de 1994 en las correspondientes a los países del norte de América, Asia Oriental y Oceanía. El aumento de los costes, sobre todo en lo referente al papel y a la distribución, hacen obligatoria esta revisión tarifaria, que contempla un incremento del 11,1% en los precios que han permanecido sin cambios durante más tiempo y menor en las tarifas que fueron modificadas en abril de 1994. El precio del ejemplar suelto de venta al número pasa a ser de $2,25. El nuevo cuadro de tarifas de suscripción queda fijado como sigue:

NUEVAS TARIFAS DE LA EDICIÓN INTERNACIONAL

Destino	US $ 1 año (52 números)	US $ 9 meses (39 números)	US $ 6 meses (26 números)	US $ 3 meses (13 números)
EE UU y Canadá	105	80	55	30
Asia oriental y Oceanía	125	95	65	35
Resto de países	100	75	50	25

23 This announcement informs readers that

1 subscribers will receive additional copies at no cost
2 an international edition will soon be available
3 subscription prices will be raised
4 more copies will be printed each day

A los santiagueros sólo les resta llorar por su ciudad. Han resultado inútiles todos los esfuerzos que ha hecho la prensa y las amas de casas para mantener limpia la ciudad de Santiago.

Santiago se ha convertido en una ciudad altamente contaminada, con una fea imagen por la basura que anda por dondequiera.

Los escasos camiones recolectores de basura que le quedan al Ayuntamiento de la ciudad están deteriorados.

En las zonas céntricas de la ciudad pasan cada diez o quince días a recoger la basura y los desperdicios que se amontonan en la ciudad. En los barrios periféricos la ausencia es mayor.

La ciudadanía aprende a no lanzar desperdicios a las calles. Pero hace falta el rigor de la ley para disciplinar a los insensatos que todavía echan basura en la ciudad.

A los santiagueros sólo les resta llorar por el abandono de su otrora ciudad limpia y organizada.

El autor es abogado

24 According to this editorial, the city of Santiago has a problem with

1 repairing public streets
2 inadequate garbage removal
3 deterioration of the city hall
4 excessive automobile traffic

UNO DE LOS ALIMENTOS QUE MEJOR RESPONDE A LAS NECESIDADES DE LOS HOGARES DE HOY

Cada vez somos más los que tendemos a llevar una alimentación sana y equilibrada. Y cada vez es menos el tiempo del que disponemos para preparar platos realmente sanos, nutritivos y atractivos para toda la familia.

Con los seis sabores de Gelatina Royal-Naranja, Limón, Fresa, Piña, Frambuesa y Tutti Frutti- o en su variedad de Gelatina Neutra Royal, se pueden hacer deliciosas y espectaculares recetas, preparándolas en un momento y dejándolas en el frigorífico (mínimo dos horas) antes de sorprender a grandes y pequeños con un desayuno, postre, merienda o cena excepcionales a la vista, suaves y frescos al paladar, y muy saludables.

25 This advertisement is intended to appeal to

1 teachers of health courses
2 families who want to buy a refrigerator
3 people interested in fast ways of cooking
4 families with health problems

(c) Directions (26–30): In the following passage there are five blank spaces numbered 26 through 30. Each blank space represents a missing word or expression. For each blank space, four possible completions are provided. Only one of them makes sense *in the context of the passage.*

First, read the passage in its entirety to determine its general meaning. Then read it a second time. For each blank space, choose the completion that makes the best sense and write its *number* in the space provided on your answer sheet. [10]

Puerto Rico: Isla Turística

Al ponerse el sol sobre las altas montañas de la Cordillera Central de Puerto Rico, los techos rojos de Hacienda Juanita brillan en medio de la vegetación tropical. El patio central de la Hacienda Juanita es un refugio tranquilo con una plaza, una fuente y flores vibrantes. El aire fresco y los colores pastel le dan al comedor un ambiente agradable.

La Hacienda Juanita fue establecida hace más de 150 años por un aristócrata español. La tierra era fértil para establecer una plantación de café. Hoy día la Hacienda Juanita es uno de los destinos turísticos más especiales de la isla. La Hacienda es parte del sistema de paradores de Puerto Rico. Los paradores, o posadas, son hoteles pequeños con un espíritu particular. Los paradores se encuentran en los lugares menos visitados de la isla por los turistas. La Hacienda Juanita y los otros ___(26)___ están ganando popularidad con los turistas que están cansados de los grandes hoteles. Estos ___(27)___ están ansiosos de escapar de la multitud para explorar los variados encantos del campo puertorriqueño.

Según María Alicia Laird, una turista que viajó allí de Nueva York, la Hacienda Juanita provee una experiencia típica de esta bella isla. En la Hacienda "hay un verdadero deseo de preservar lo que es auténticamente ___(28)___. El menú es muy típico. La piscina es una maravilla. La librería y la tienda de regalos tienen cosas auténticas. ¡Nos encantó!"

En otros lugares de la isla, el sistema de paradores que son administrados por el gobierno ofrece experiencias similares. Otra posada llamada Villa Parguera, al sudoeste de la isla, combina las comodidades de un gran hotel con la atmósfera de informalidad de un parador. "Hay gente que viene cada año desde hace 25 años", dice el gerente, Nelson Ortega. "Tenemos un ___(29)___ familar que se adapta perfectamente para cualquiera, desde parejas de Luna de Miel hasta ancianos".

Una de las atracciones del lugar es el maravilloso espectáculo nocturno en la Bahía Fosforescente. Otro lugar para visitar está a apenas 20 minutos. Se trata del pueblo de Cabo Rojo, con sus acantilados lisos, sus olas fuertes y un faro construido en estilo español.

Cerca de la ciudad de Coamo, el Parador Baños de Coamo refleja la elegancia que cultivaba décadas atrás, con los baños termales más exclusivos de la isla. Las aguas termales y el ambiente rural con aspectos coloniales hace del Parador Baños de Coamo uno de los paradores más ____(30)____.

A la sombra de la montaña más alta de Puerto Rico en la ciudad de Jayuya, la Hacienda Gripiñas es otro de los paradores históricos. La vieja finca de café de la Hacienda Gripiñas está rodeada de palmeras. El terreno cuidadosamente mantenido da la imagen de elegancia ganada con esfuerzo.

Luis Rivera, dueño de la Hacienda Juanita dice que "En España, los paradores usualmente están en viejos castillos. Pero en Puerto Rico no usamos los castillos como paradores, pero sí tenemos un encanto que es únicamente nuestro".

(26) 1 comedores
     2 paradores
     3 lagos
     4 terrenos

(27) 1 visitantes
     2 nativos
     3 trabajadores
     4 estudiantes

(28) 1 puertorriqueño
     2 neoyorquino
     3 americano
     4 internacional

(29) 1 número
     2 país
     3 ambiente
     4 mercado

(30) 1 complicados
     2 baratos
     3 aburridos
     4 atractivos

PART 3

Write your answers to Part 3 according to the directions for *a* and *b*. [16]

(*a*) *Directions:* In your answer booklet, write **one** well-organized note in Spanish as directed below. [6]

Choose **either** question 31 **or** 32. Write the number of the question you have chosen in the space provided on your answer sheet. Write a well-organized note, following the specific instructions given in the question you have chosen. Your note must consist of **at least six clauses**. To qualify for credit, a clause must contain a verb, a stated or implied subject, and additional words necessary to convey meaning. The six clauses may be contained in fewer than six sentences if some of the sentences have more than one clause.

---

31 You are an exchange student in Venezuela and have been asked by a teacher at your host school to talk to students about your own school in New York State. Write a note in Spanish to that teacher responding to the teacher's request.

In the note, you may want to thank the teacher for the opportunity to talk about your school and indicate whether you will be able to carry out the teacher's request. If you are unable to talk to students, you may wish to express your regret and tell why you cannot do what was requested. You may also want to make an alternate suggestion. If you are able to talk to students, you may wish to mention what topics you would like to talk about (e.g., use of time, food, music, school activities), ask your teacher any questions you have about the request, and indicate how much time you need to prepare. Your may also wish to suggest a time and place for this activity. **Be sure to accomplish the purpose of the note, which is *to respond to the teacher's request.***

Use the following:

Salutation: Estimado Profesor/ Estimada Profesora,
Closing: [your name]

The salutation and closing will *not* be counted as part of the six required clauses.

32 Your teacher gave everyone in your class a different assignment to complete. You do not like your topic and want to change it. Write a note in Spanish to your teacher to request a change in the topic.

In the note, you may wish to explain why you do not like the topic that was assigned and what topic you want to be assigned and why (e.g., availability of sources for references, familiarity with the topic, interest in the topic). You may also want to express your appreciation for considering your request to change the topic. **Be sure to accomplish the purpose of the note, which is *to request a change in the topic*.**

Use the following:

Salutation: Estimado/Estimada [teacher's name],
Closing: Su estudiante, [your name]

The salutation and closing will *not* be counted as part of the six required clauses.

(*b*) *Directions:* On your answer sheet, write **one** well-organized composition in Spanish as directed below.   [10]

Choose **either** question 33 **or** 34. Write the number of the question you have chosen in the space provided on your answer sheet. Write a well-organized composition, following the specific instructions given in the question you have chosen. Your composition must consist of **at least 10 clauses**. To qualify for credit, a clause must contain a verb, a stated or implied subject, and additional words necessary to convey meaning. The 10 clauses may be contained in fewer than 10 sentences if some of the sentences have more than one clause.

---

33 In Spanish, write a story about the situation shown in the picture below. It must be a story relating to the picture, **not** a description of the picture. Do *not* write a dialogue.

34   Your Spanish Club is planning a trip to Mexico during summer vacation. You are responsible for getting information in order to help plan the trip. In Spanish, write a letter to the Mexican Embassy requesting information.

You must accomplish the purpose of the letter, which is *to request information about Mexico*.

In your letter, you may want to ask about places and sites to visit, accommodations, weather, appropriate dress, public transportation, special events, and festivals. You may also wish to mention when you will take the trip and how you feel about going.

You may use any or all of the ideas suggested above or you may use your own ideas. **Either way, you must request information about Mexico**.

Use the following:

Dateline: el 27 de enero de 1999
Salutation: Estimado Director/Estimada Directora,
Closing: Atentamente, [your name]
The dateline, salutation, and closing will *not* be counted as part of the 10 required clauses.

LISTENING COMPREHENSION
PART 1A

Listening Comprehension: The following passages should be read aloud to the students during Part 1A. The background information should be read in English *once*, the passages should each be read in Spanish *twice*, and the question should be read in English *once*. Do not allow more than one minute between questions. [30]

---

1 A Spanish-speaking celebrity is being interviewed on television. She says:

   Yo era una niña como todas, con mucha fantasía y tenía el gran sueño de ser pintora. Hija de padre chino y madre cubana, yo contemplaba con deleite mi mundo lleno de color que deseaba con fuerza en imágenes.

   As a child, what did this celebrity always want to do?

2 You are at the airport in Cancun, Mexico, and hear this announcement:

   Señores y Señoras. Es prohibido llevar frutas o vegetales de México a los Estados Unidos. Todos los pasajeros deben abordar el avión sin productos cultivados en México. La aduana en los Estados Unidos va a confiscar alimentos de este país traídos por los turistas y también les pondrá una multa.

   What information does this announcement give to tourists?

3 You are at a shopping mall and hear this announcement over the public address system:

   Cambio 16, fiel a su cita, ofrece a los hombres todo lo que necesitan saber para estar a la última moda esta primavera-verano en el extra Moda 16. En esta edición especial hablamos de las tendencias en la moda de baño; los colores blancos, crudos y tostados, protagonistas de la temporada; la nueva ropa interior; los cuidados personales o los movimientos que marcan el estilo nuevo en la decoración. Por eso, Cambio 16 cuesta esta semana 475 pesetas.

   Why is a new price being advertised?

4 When you arrive home from school, you hear your Spanish friend's message on your telephone answering machine:

   Te habla, Alicia. Lo siento, pero no fui a recoger el reloj como te prometí. Escucha. Es que esta mañana mi coche no funcionó y pasé todo el día con mi papá y el mecánico. ¡Qué horror! Ya llamé al joyero para decirle que no podiá ir. Lo siento mucho. ¡Llámame cuando regreses!

   What message did Alicia leave on the answering machine?

5   A visitor has come to your Spanish class to speak about her recent trip to Belize, Central America. She says:

Este verano visité un lugar histórico maravilloso. Escondido en las junglas, existe un auténtico tesoro de ciudades mayas. Este sitio data de miles de años y empieza ahora a ser apreciado por los arqueólogos. Al visitar este lugar histórico, se hace evidente que Belice fue una vez un gran centro del Imperio Maya. Allí, pasé la mayor parte de mis vacaciones, y yo lo recomiendo a quien tenga interés en las civilizaciones antiguas.

Where did this traveler spend most of her time?

6   You are listening to a television program about famous Latin Americans and hear this information:

La actriz mexicana Angélica Rivera actúa en la telenovela "La Dueña". La telenovela que recientemente terminó ahora se transmite en otros países. Es un éxito en Chile, Puerto Rico, Perú y los Estados Unidos. Las transmisiones a estos países le han dado a esta estrella mexicana fama internacional. Ahora Angélica Rivera iniciará su carrera como modelo y conductora de programas de videos.

How did Angélica Rivera achieve international fame?

7   You are an exchange student in Spain. During your hosts' absence, you answer this call from a telephone company representative:

Hola. Soy representante de la telefónica y quisiera ofrecerles un servicio nuevo, Teletimbres. Este servicio les permite tener hasta dos números telefónicos adicionales en su línea. Los números, aunque usan sólo una línea, tienen sonidos distintos. Así, el sonido del teléfono indicará para quién es la llamada antes de descolgar.

What does this message concern?

8   Your Spanish teacher is telling the class about an unusual "festival" in Spain. She says:

En Buñol, un pequeño pueblo en el este de España, se celebra "la tomatina" el último miércoles de agosto. No es una fiesta religiosa, sino un corto tiempo de gozo en tirarse tomates. Camiones llenos de tomates bien maduros pasan por la calle y reparten tomates a la gente, especialmente entre los chicos jóvenes. Con mucha risa, todos se tiran los tomates que vuelan por todas partes. "La tomatina" comienza y termina según un horario estricto y con reglas de cuidado. Dos horas después de tirarse el último tomate, la calle está tan limpia como si nunca hubiera ocurrido esta diversión.

How would visitors to this small village in Spain participate in its festival?

9   While shopping in a supermarket in Mexico, you hear this advertisement:

"Comebien", una marca líder en Europa, garantiza que sus productos son sanos y mantienen el sabor original y la riqueza en nutrientes. Estos productos son naturales y, además, protegen y cuidan el medio ambiente. Se nota que no utilizan los elementos químicos que contaminan los alimentos y que destruyen la riqueza de la tierra.

What new type of product is being made available to consumers?

PART 1B

The following passages should be read aloud to the students during Part 1B. The background information should be read in English *once*, the passages should each be read in Spanish *twice* and the question should be read in Spanish *once*. Do not allow more than one minute between questions.

---

10   While in Madrid, you hear a sports commentator on television. He says:

El origen de las gorras de béisbol fue muy práctico: para proteger a lso jugadores do los rayos del sol. Pero pronto se han hecho populares las gorras en otros deportes. Hoy día la fabricación y comercialización de gorras deportivas es un negocio de primera magnitud. Ahora cuestan entre 1.850 pesetas y 15.000 pesetas. Las gorras más deseables son las de los Yankees de Nueva York y las de los White Sox de Chicago.

¿De qué trata este anuncio?

11   Your friend is telling you about a way to relax. Your friend says:

Yo trabajo como secretaria bilingue en una agencia internacional. Como pueden imaginarse siempre tengo mucho que hacer. A veces quiero dejarlo todo y salir corriendo. Los únicos momentos en que me siento aliviada, son cuando leo mi nueva edición de VANIDADES. Cada página de esta revista es una sorpresa agradable para mí; siempre la leo toda, incluyendo la sección de correspondencia y sé que reciben miles de felicitaciones, las cuales apoyo sinceramente.

¿Cómo se escapa tu amiga de su rutina en el trabajo?

12   You are listening to the radio and hear this advertisement:

Los largos viajes por carretera serán más agradables gracias al sistema multimedia Clarión para el automóvil. Detrás del asiento del conductor se instala un televisor a color de 15 centímetros, con vídeo, para que los viajeros del coche disfruten de los largos viajes. Por sólo 250.000 pesetas los viajeros pueden disfrutar de juegos en la televisión o ver sus películas favoritas.

¿Qué beneficio ofrece el sistema Clarión?

13   You are talking to your friend Geraldo from Bolivia. He tells you about what happened to him last night at the movies. He says:

Le pedí a una señora que estaba sentada delante de mí si sería tan amable de quitarse el sombrero. Ella me dijo en tono violento que si no podiá ver que me sentara en otro lugar. como el cine estaba bastante lleno decidí quedarme donde estaba porque no íbamos a conseguir otros asientos para sentarnos todos juntos. Así que no pude disfrutar mucho la película.

¿Por qué no pudo disfrutar la película Geraldo?

14   Your are listening to the radio in Lima, Peru, and you hear this advertisement:

Si tus dientes no están blancos es porque tú no quieres. Blanx, el nuevo producto dentifrico, reúne dos conceptos en un solo producto: salud y belleza para tus dientes. Blanx es el primer dentífrico cosmético protector que blanquea tus dientes naturalmente. Contiene una sustancia natural, y previene la formación de las caries. El blanco natural de tus dientes volverá. Es hora de que regrese el blanco de tus dientes. Blanx, dientes blanco, dientes sanos y de forma natural.

¿Cuál es una ventaja de este producto?

15   You are walking on a street in Barcelona and you hear Graciela and Rosa talking. Rosa says:

Oye, estoy harta de caminar. No conozco esta ciudad para nada. Hace media hora que caminamos y no encontramos el restaurante. Dices que estaba en esta esquina, pero ya le hemos dado la vuelta a la manzana varias veces y no lo vimos. Vamos a preguntarle a alguien porque si no, vamos a llegar tarde a la cita.

¿Qué problema tienen Graciela y Rosa?

ANSWER BOOKLET
FOR
COMPREHENSIVE EXAMINATION
IN SPANISH

Student: .... Sex: ☐ Male ☐ Female

Teacher: ....

School: ....

City: ....

Part 1				
a 1..........	4..........	7..........	*b* 10..........	13..........
2..........	5..........	8..........	11..........	14..........
3..........	6..........	9..........	12..........	15..........

Credit

[a]

[OVER]

Part 2

a 16 .... b 21 .... c 26 ....

17 ....   22 ....   27 ....

18 ....   23 ....   28 ....

19 ....   24 ....   29 ....

20 ....   25 ....   30 ....

Credit

Part 3*a*

Question Number _____

....

....

....

....

....

....

....

....

....

....

....

....

....

....

....

[b]

Part 3*b*

Question Number _____

....

....

....

....

....

....

....

....

....

....

....

....

....

....

....

....

....

Total Checks (4*a* + 4*b*): _____ /3 = Credit

[c]

Sample Test I
Answers and
Explanations

ANSWER KEY

1A	1B	2A	2B	2C
1. 1	10. 4	16. 2	21. 1	26. 2
2. 3	11. 2	17. 3	22. 4	27. 1
3. 4	12. 3	18. 2	23. 3	28. 1
4. 4	13. 1	19. 1	24. 2	29. 3
5. 2	14. 2	20. 4	25. 3	30. 4
6. 2	15. 2			
7. 3				
8. 1				
9. 3				

ANSWERS AND EXPLANATIONS

PART 1A

1　**1**　"...tenía el gran sueño de ser pintora."

　　2　She mentions that her father is Chinese and her mother Cuban, but she doesn't say that she wants to visit other countries.

　　3　She says nothing about performing in the theatre.

　　4　She says nothing about learning other languages.

2　**1**　The announcement declares that it is illegal to bring fruit and vegetables from Mexico into the United States.

　　2　Food is mentioned, but not because it will be served on the flight.

　　3　"La aduana en los Estados Unidos va a confiscar alimentos de este país traídos por los turistas y tambíen les pondrá una multa."

　　4　Passengers and boarding are mentioned, but young children or the boarding order are not.

3　**1**　The announcement does not discuss mailing costs.

　　2　The announcement mentions the spring-summer issue, but no delay in production.

　　3　Labor is not discussed.

　　4　"Cambio 16, fiel a su cita, ofrece a los hombres todo lo que necesitan saber para estar a la última moda esta primavera-verano en el extra Moda 16...Por eso, Cambio 16 cuesta esta semana 475 pesetas."

4　**1**　She did not forget about the watch. She even says that despite her car problems she remembered to call the jeweler.

　　2　The jeweler is mentioned, but we can not assume that she did not have the gift ready.

　　3　Her father was with her at the mechanic because the car had mechanical problems, not because he borrowed the automobile.

　　4　"Lo siento, pero no fui a recoger el reloj como te prometí."

5　**1**　She was in Belize, but she spent her time in ruins hidden in the jungles, not at the beach.

　　2　"...existe un auténtico tesoro de ciudades mayas. Este sitio data de miles de años...Allí pase la mayor parte de mis vacaciones."

　　3　She discusses Belize's importance as a historical place, but she wasn't shopping there.

　　4　She visited ruins in the jungle, not museums.

6 1 The program says that her career started with modeling work, but we are looking for the manner in which she became an international star.

2 "...actua en la telenovela 'La Dueña'...Es un éxito en Chile, Puerto Rico, Perú, y los Estados Unidos."

3 The very last line says that she was a *director* of video programs. Don't confuse *conductora* with "conductor" in English.

4 Angélica Rivera is Mexican, but appearing in commercials is not the reason she has achieved international fame.

7 1 This is an offer related to telephone service, but nothing is mentioned about disconnecting your host's service.

2 The offer is for additional service, not an answering machine.

3 "Este servicio les permite tener hasta dos números telefónicos adicionales en su línea."

4 Most likely anyone who decides to add this service will experience a change in their phone rate; however, the service itself is the focus of the call.

8 1 "Con mucha risa, todos se tiran los tomates..."

2 Although parades are common to festivals and celebrations, this unique festival does not involve one.

3 Don't be thrown off by the inclusion of tomatoes in the description of the festival. Food is thrown, not eaten here.

4 The teacher says there are people in the streets, but they are throwing tomatoes, not dancing.

9 1 The advertisement does not say anything about the products being grown in water instead of soil. In fact, it says that their products do not use chemicals that destroy the soil.

2 It is possible that these products are vitamins, but the passage does not state this. Don't make any assumptions; keep looking for a better answer.

3 "...garantiza que sus productos son sanos...Estos productos son naturales."

4 The advertisement does not discuss preparation techniques for their products.

PART 1B

10 1 The announcement discusses baseball caps (*gorras*), not tickets to baseball games.

2 The announcement says nothing of a lack of respect concerning baseball fans.

3 The announcement does mention manufacturing, but again, he is discussing baseball hats, not aluminum bats.

4 "Pero pronto se han hecho populares las gorras...Hoy día la fabricación y comercialización de gorras deportivas es un negocio de primera magnitud."

11 1 Although talking on the telephone is a very logical and common way to escape the daily routine of work, it is not your friend's method.

2 Los únicos momentos en que me siento aliviada, son cuando leo mi nueva edición de VANIDADES.

3 She doesn't say anything about her personal mail.

4 Again, listening to your favorite music is a common way to make work more agreeable, but it is not the method your friend chooses.

12 1 You might be tempted to choose this one because the passage is about enhancing the experience of taking long road trips, but the service offered benefits the passengers, not the driver.

2 The radio advertisement does not mention accidents.

3 "...para que los viajeros del coche disfruten de los largos viajes...los viajeros pueden disfrutar de juegos en la televisión o ver sus películas favoritas."

4 Pollution reduction is a logical choice for a passage about long car trips, but don't be tricked into selecting this choice.

13 **1 "Le pedí a una señora que estaba sentada delante de mí si sería tan amable de quitarse el sombrero. Ella me dijo...que si no podía ver que me sentara en otro lugar." (This one is a little tricky, but you should have recognized that he couldn't see because his view was blocked by the woman's hat.)**

2 Geraldo does talk about the seating in the theater, but he says it is crowded. This is a tempting answer, but choice 1 is better.

3 The woman spoke to him in a violent tone, but it is her hat that causes the problem.

4 He doesn't say anything about whether or not he can hear the film.

14 1 The ad mentions cavities (*caries*), but alleviating pain is not the main selling point of the product.

2 **"Contiene una sustancia natural...El blanco de tus dientes volvereá."**

3 Bad breath (*el mal aliento*) is not mentioned in the ad.

4 The ad does not say that *Blanco* eliminated the need to brush your teeth.

15 1 Rosa does not mention money. Keep looking for a better answer.

2 **"Oye, estoy harta (I am tired of) de caminar. No conozco esta ciudad para nada."**

3 No, in fact the last sentence says that she will be late.

4 She does not mention taking the bus.

PART 2A

16 2 *Paragraph 5, lines 2-3*
"En este punto de mi vida decidí cambiar de carrera. Yo dejé de ser soldado y empecé a escribir."

17 3 *Paragraph 3, lines 4-5*
"Perdí el uso de la mano izquierda y por eso me llaman el Manco de Lepanto."

18 2 *Paragraph 7, line 1*
"Estaba yo entonces enamorado de Catalina Salazar y Palacios. Me casé con ella…"

19 1 *Paragraph 8, lines 1-2*
" Que días más tristes pasé en la cárcel! Pero, allí empece a escribir mi primera novela, *El ingenioso hidalgo don Quijote de La Mancha, también conocido como Don Quijote.*"

20 4 *Paragraph 10, lines 1-2*
"Es verdad que mi vida era difícil, pero mis dificultades me hicieron filósofo. Mis aventuras fueron la materia que les dio vida a mis narraciones."

PART 2B

21 1 "Gracias a **Inglés Sin Barreras**, el curso de inglés americano con explicaciones en español."

2 You might be tempted to selct this answer because the ad mentions television, but it doesn't say anything about repairing TVs.

3 Don't be duped into picking this answer. The ad sells the idea of using tapes for educational purposes, but they can be used in a car, at home, or at work, not in a classroom.

4 These are educational videocassettes, not recordings of popular music.

22 1 and 2—The first sentence and the headline, ¡*ALERTA!*, should tip you off that the subject matter is something more important than dressing children in practical clothing or developing their artistic talents.

3 This is a more logical choice, but the overwhelming amount of advice pertains to thoroughly checking out the modeling agency.

4 The entire bulleted list involves methods of investigating the credentials of modeling agencies.

23 1 Subscriptions are mentioned, but the headline and first sentence should tip you off that there is a better answer.

2 The international edition of *El Pais* already exists, it is nothing new.

3 "...la Edición Internacional de El País va a aumentar sus tarifas generales, tanto de suscripción como del precio de portada."

4 Refer to the headline for the main subject of the article. It is about a price increase, not an increase in printing.

24 1 The editorial discusses a problem with the streets of Santiago, but the problem is the amount of garbage in the streets, not their condition.

2 "Los escasos camiones recolectores de basura que le quedan al Ayuntamiento de la ciudad están deteriorados."

3 Deterioration and the poor image of the city is mentioned, but the main problem here is garbage.

4 Again, garbage is the problem in Santiago.

25 1 Health plays a role in the advertisement, but the target audience is not teachers.

2 Refer to the headline. Does it make sense that an advertisement for a refrigerator, starts with a headline about a food? Keep looking for a better answer.

3 "Y cada vez es menos el tiempo del que disponemos para preparar platos sanos, nutritivos y atractivos para toda la familia."

4 You might be tempted to go with this one because the ad mentions *Gelatina Royal's* health benefits, but the beginning of the ad states that everyone needs nutritious food, not just families with health problems.

PART 2C

26 **2** In the sentences preceding the answer blank, the *Hacienda Juanita* is described as being a part of the system of *paradores* (defined as small, but distinctive hotels) in Puerto Rico. You should have remembered to look back in the sentences before the blank for the information you need to choose the best answer.

27 **1** Again, look at the sentences before the one that contains the blank. You should remember that the passage is about tourism, so you can eliminate *trabajadores* (workers) and *estudiantes* (students). The sentence with the blank contains the verbs *escapar* (to escape) and *explorar* (to explore), which are very similar in spelling to their English counterparts. Make use of such words wherever you can, they are your best friends on this test. Are *nativos* or *visitantes* more likely to be associated with these activities?

28 **1** This blank also has words that are very close to their English counterparts. "Hay un verdadero deseo de *preservar* lo que es *autenticamente...*" This time the sentence following the blank offers help: "El *menú* es muy *típico.*" There should be little doubt that the hotel is authentically **Puerto Rican**.

29 **3** The sentences before the one with the blank should tip you off that the passage is discussing the ambience of the *Villa Paraguera*. You can also try the other answer choices to make sure that *ambiente* is the best one. "We have a familiar *number, country, or market...*" None of these make as much sense as **ambiance**.

30 **4** The paragraph describes the selling points of the *Parador Banos de Coama*. To fill in the blank you should be able to deduce that all these factors combine to make this hotel one of the most **attractive** on the island. The other choices, *complicados, baratos,* and *aburridos* don't make nearly as much sense.

PART 3A

31 Sample note:

Estimado Profesor,

Muchas gracias por la oportunidad de discutir acerca de mi escuela en Nueva York./ Tengo muchas ganas de hablar sobre las diferencias entre Nueva York y Caracas(Venezuela). / Es posible que use fotos para ilustrar mi discusión/ Quiero hablar también sobre mis experiencias con el equipo de fútbol americano y el campamento del fin de semana. / Tal vez haga mi presentación la semana próxima.

Su estudiante,

Jorge

32 Sample note:

Estimada Sra. González,

Le escribo esta carta porque tengo problemas con mi proyecto de fin de año./ No tengo ninguna experiencia con el tema del oeste de los Estados Unidos./ No creo que pueda conseguir suficiente información para terminarlo a tiempo/ He buscado en la biblioteca y no hay muchos libros sobre este tema./ Prefiero otro tópico, como por ejemplo la guerra en Chiapas./ Hay muchos artículos en los periódicos/y además es un tema de mucha actualidad/ Muchas gracias por considerar mi petición.

Su estudiante,

Carla

PART 3B

33   Sample composition:

*33 Cada día Miguel destruye algo en su casa./ No lo hace a propósito./ En
una semana Miguel rompió todas las lamparas de la sala./ Sus padres tienen
paciencia con él/ pero la conducta destructiva de Miguel es muy costosa./ Un
día su madre volvió de trabajar/ y Miguel habia roto la lampara favorita de su
madre./ Era una reliquia familiar./ La madre decidió llevar a Miguel a ver a un
siquiatra./ El siquiatra dijo que Miguel miraba demasiada televisión violenta.*

34   Sample composition:

Estimado Director,   *27 de enero de 1999*

*Mi nombre es Michael Oakes. Soy estudiante de secundaria en los Estados
Unidos./ Mi club de español va a viajar a México esta primavera./ Quisiera
alguna información sobre el estado de Yucatán./ Yo sé que hay muchos hoteles
allí/ pero desearía saber si hay otros sitios para hospedarnos./ Cuales son las
principales atracciones de Yucatán/ En especial desearía visitar las ruinas de
los Maya./ Además quiero saber si hay fiestas importantes durante esta
temporada./ ¿Cómo es el clima?/ ¿Podremos nadar en el mar?/ ¿Necesitamos
viajar por autobús o taxi hasta Yucatán? Estoy muy emocionado por este
viaje./ Muchas gracias por su ayuda/ y espero conocerlo muy pronto.*

Atentamente,

Juan Carlos

Sample Test II

PART 1

Answer all questions in Part 1 according to the directions for *a* and *b*.

Listening Comprehension passages begin on page 217.

(*a*) *Directions* (1–9): For each question, you will hear some background information in English *once*. Then you will hear a passage in Spanish *twice* and a question in English *once*. After you have heard the question, the teacher will pause while you read the question and the four suggested answers on your test. Choose the best suggested answer and write its *number* in the space provided on your answer sheet. Base you answer *on the content of the passage, only*.   [18]

---

1 What will take place this afternoon?

    1 a field trip to a local theater
    2 tryouts for the basketball team
    3 a presentation by the principal
    4 a meeting about a school play

2 What is required to purchase one of these dolls?

    1 a toy that can be recycled
    2 a photograph of the child
    3 a pediatrician's prescription
    4 a monetary contribution to charity

3 What did Steven Fisher discover?

    1 the purpose of the wooden tablets
    2 the importance of languages
    3 the meaning of some writings
    4 the first person to inhabit Easter Island.

4 What does this advertisement offer?

    1 an opportunity to change careers
    2 an opportunity to spend a vacation helping others
    3 special rates for traveling around the country
    4 special classes to improve your Spanish

5   What information does the news report give?
    1   the latest plan to reduce smog
    2   the personal health dangers of smog
    3   the daily smog level advisory
    4   the rise in the level of contamination of crops by smog

6   What kind of work are these volunteers expected to do?
    1   provide food for the children's programs
    2   work in the gift shop
    3   provide transportation to the office
    4   help with the cleanup

7   What does the desk clerk explain to the tourist?
    1   the itinerary for the trip
    2   the hours of departure from the hotel
    3   information about exchanging money
    4   the price of 4- and 5-star hotels in Madrid

8   What is unusual about this restaurant?
    1   It never closes.
    2   It is covered with exotic flowers.
    3   It serves tapas.
    4   It serves meals in the pool.

9   According to this lecturer, where did the game of chess originate?
    1   Spain
    2   Persia
    3   Arabia
    4   India

(b) *Directions* (10–15): For each question, you will hear some background information in English *once*. Then you will hear a passage in Spanish *twice* and a question in Spanish *once*. After you have heard the question, the teacher will pause while you read the question and the four suggested answers on your test. Choose the best suggested answer and write its *number* in the space provided on your answer sheet. Base your answer *on the content of the passage, only*. [12]

10   ¿De qué se trata este anuncio?

   1   una fiesta en el restaurante "El gato negro"
   2   dos famosas orquestas de música salsa
   3   un disco compacto nuevo del cantante Gilberto Santarosa
   4   un menú especial de la región

11   ¿Qué es la Puerta del Sol?

   1   una obra teatral madrileña
   2   un museo famoso
   3   un centro de mucha actividad
   4   una época histórica

12   ¿Qué dice el guía de la ciudad de San Juan?

   1   Allí se encuentran varios tipos de arquitectura
   2   Ponce de León destruyó la vieja ciudad.
   3   La playa está muy lejos de la ciudad.
   4   Todos los edificios son modernísimos.

13 ¿Qué se le ofrece al pasajero?
    1 revistas internacionales para leer
    2 programación para todos los gustos de música
    3 unos ejercicios para hacer durante el vuelo
    4 unas películas para niños

14 ¿Qué es Nueva Dermis?
    1 un programa que cambia lo que va a comer
    2 un tratamiento para mantener sano el pelo
    3 unas clínicas famosas que acaban de abrir en España
    4 un plan para mejorar el aspecto de la piel de la cara

15 ¿Qué información da este anuncio?
    1 Quiere comentarios sobre el servicio ofrecido.
    2 Informa donde recoger el equipaje.
    3 Anuncia nuevas rutas y mejores precios.
    4 Aconseja a los pasajeros que siempre vuelen
       por Avianca.

PART 2

Answer all questions in Part 2 according to the directions for *a*, *b*, and *c*.   [30]

(*a*) *Directions* (16–20): After the following passage, there are five questions or incomplete statements. For *each*, choose the word or expression that best answers the question or completes the statement *according to the meaning of the passage*, and write its *number* in the space provided on your answer sheet.   [10]

Alcanzando las Estrellas

Como muchos niños que se criaron en los años 50 y 60, Franklin Chang Díaz soñaba con ser astronauta. La guerra fría había hecho de la conquista del espacio una carrera en la que parecía que todo el mundo tenía algo que ganar, o perder. Cuando miraba hacia el cielo desde San José, Costa Rica, Franklin Chang Díaz no se imaginaba que sería uno de los primeros hispanoamericanos en viajar al espacio.

Cuando tenía 9 años, Franklin Chang Díaz construyó su propia nave espacial usando una silla de la cocina y una caja de cartón. A los 15 años, el ingenioso joven diseñó un cohete mecánico y lo disparó hacia el cielo con un pobre ratoncito amarrado a la cabina delantera. "Parecía que había subido muchísimo, llegando a la estratosfera, pero seguramente no llegó a más de 100 pies". (No se preocupen, el ratón regresó a la tierra sano y salvo gracias a un paracaídas.)

Hoy día, los cohetes y el espacio no son juegos de niños para este astronauta de la NASA. Chang Díaz, de 49 años, es el astronauta hispanoamericano más destacado de la NASA y el primer director latino del Laboratorio de Propulsión Avanzada de la NASA en Houston. En 1986, Chang Díaz se convirtió en el primer hispanoamericano en viajar en el transbordador espacial y ahora está trabajando en el proyecto más importante de su vida: el motor de una nave espacial que llevará a personas al planeta Marte. "El espacio siempre me fascinó", recuerda. "Fue mi sueño".

Luchar por sus sueños es parte de la tradición familiar de Chang Díaz. A principios del siglo XX, su abuelo paterno, José Chang, emigró de la China en busca de una vida mejor en Costa Rica. Su abuelo materno, Roberto Díaz, vivió en los Estados unidos durante 20 años trabajando con la marina mercante, antes de regresar a su país natal, Costa Rica. "Mi familia es una familia de inmigrantes", dice Franklin, cuyo nombre de pila fue inspirado por el presidente estadounidense Franklin Delano Roosevelt, a quién su abuelo Díaz admiraba mucho. "Mi abuelo siempre me dijo que si quería lograr mis sueños tenía que ir a los Estados Unidos".

Pero sus sueños no se iban a realizar tan fácilmente. Hijo de Ramón, un jefe de construcción, y María Eugenia, una a ma de casa, Franklin se crió junto a sus cinco hermanos en una modesta casa colonial. A los 18 años, viajó a los Estados Unidos con sólo $50 en el bolsillo y, como muchos latinos, fue a quedarse en casa de un primo lejano que vivía con sus nueve hijos en un pequeño apartamento en Hartford, Connecticut. "Sé que yo era una carga para ellos, pero no tenía más remedio".

Aunque ya se había graduado de la escuela secundaria en Costa Rica, Franklin se matriculó en una escuela pública de Hartford para aprender inglés. Tan buenas fueron sus notas al hacer la secundaria en inglés, que se ganó una beca de un año para empezar sus estudios en la Universidad de Connecticut. "Esa ayuda económica era lo que yo necesitaba y de allí, mi carrera se encaminó".

Hoy, Franklin ayuda a encaminar a otros, aconsejando a jóvenes estudiantes sobre oportunidades en la NASA. Y tampoco quiere que sus hijos se olviden de sus raíces. "El no habla conmigo si no es en español", dice su hija Lidia.

Aunque Franklin tiene una gran colección de trofeos y títulos, su orgullo es la Medalla de la Libertad que le fue otorgada por el ex presidente Ronald Reagan en 1986. "Esa es la más importante porque reconoce las contribuciones de un inmigrante a los Estados Unidos", dice Franklin.

16 Desde su juventud se podía notar que Franklin Chang Díaz

    1 se interesaba por el espacio
    2 no tenía habilidad mecánica
    3 quería trabajar con su familia
    4 tenía muchos juguetes

17 ¿Por qué es conocido Franklin Chang Díaz?

   1 Viene de una familia con influencia política.
   2 Tiene una larga tradición de científicos en su familia.
   3 Llegó a dirigir un programa espacial norteamericano.
   4 Era una autor célebre de ciencia ficción en Costa Rica.

18 ¿Qué tiene en común Franklin Chang Díaz con sus abuelos?

   1 Todos asistieron a la misma universidad.
   2 Ellos eran de Hartford, Connecticut.
   3 Comenzaron por trabajar en construcción.
   4 Tuvieron que trabajar mucho para realizar sus sueños.

19 Según Franklin, ¿qué le ayudó a comenzar su carrera?

   1 Vio un programa de televisión sobre el espacio.
   2 Ganó un concurso científico.
   3 Recibió asistencia financiera para ir a la universidad.
   4 Trabajó para una compañia de construcción.

20 Según Franklin, ¿por qué es importante la Medalla de la Libertad?

   1 Es necesario para luchar por la libertad de expresión.
   2 Es la evidencia que los inmigrantes ofrecen mucho al país adoptado.
   3 Simboliza el fin de la guerra fría.
   4 Pone énfasis en la cooperación internacional.

(b) Directions (21–25): Below each of the following selections, there is either a question or an incomplete statement. For *each*, choose the word or expression that best answers the question or completes the statement *according to the meaning of the selection*, and write its *number* in the space provided on your answer sheet.

Llevará su 'Amor' a Caracas

CARACAS (NTX).- El internacional cantante mexicano Emmanuel llegará el próximo 9 de octubre a la capital venezolana para promocionar su más reciente producción discográfica, informaron hoy fuentes locales del espectáculo.

Emmanuel promocionará en la radio, televisión y medios impresos de Venezuela su nuevo álbum **Amor Total**, del sello Poly-Gram, al que pertenece.

En **Amor Total**, que cuenta con la dirección del conocido productor, Manuel Alejandro, Emmanuel interpreta temas del género musical ranchero y baladas románticas como "Mi Mujer".

El artista mexicano también tiene previsto presentarse el próximo 12 de octubre en el programa **Sábado Sensacional**, uno de los más sintonizados por los televidentes venezolanos.

21 Which statement is best supported by this newspaper article?

1 Emmanuel will show his paintings in Venezuela in the fall.
2 Emmanuel will promote his new release in another country.
3 Emmanuel will begin his world tour in South America.
4 Emmanuel will play rock music in an outdoor theater.

NOTICIAS
Una de las grandes cocinas de Barcelona

En el corazón del Puerto Marítimo barcelonés, esa zona admirablemente recuperada por la ciudad con motivo de los Juegos Olímpicos del 92, el restaurante Talaia Mar (Marina, 16. ☎ 93-2219090), participado y supervisado por El Bulli de Rosas, ofrece una de las mejores cocinas de Barcelona. Carlos Abellán, como jefe de cocina, y sus colaboradores Oriol Balaguer y Sergio Arola, junto con Artur Saques, como director de sala, están dando de comer con calidad y esmero asombrosos, en una zona de ocio y esparcimiento. Detras está, sin duda, la "mano alagada" de Ferrán Adriá y Juli soler, jefe de cocina y director de sala, respectivamente, de El Bulli.

Arola consiguió el premio en el último concurso de cocineros jóvenes celebrado en Vitoria. Oriol Balaguer es, por su parte, uno de los mejores reposteros de España. Tuvimos la oportunidad de disfrutar recientemente de un menú preparado por ambos. Desde unos mejillones de Cala Montjoi en escabeche ligero y unas sardinas marineras al vinagre de frambuesa, hasta unos admirables *calçots* rebozados en tempura al estilo japonés. Luego, la menestra de verduras y legumbres en ensalada (exquisita, diez sobre diez) y el consomé frío de Jabugo, flan de *ceps*, *gelée* de frutas y ensalada de oreja de cerdo y alcachofas, todo un prodigio. A continuación, el plato que obtuvo el triunfo en Vitoria: *espardonyes* con un *rissotto* de queso Idiázabal, espárragos y vinagreta.

Para terminar, la terrina caliente de foie-gras y ave con salsade *periguex*, quizás lo menos conseguido del menú. De postre, raviolis de mango rellenos de tomate a la vainilla con sorbete de yogur y su puré de albahaca, también premio en Vitoria 96.

22 What is the topic of this article?

  1 a cruise ship
  2 the Olympic Games
  3 a cooking class
  4 a restaurant

Estimado Sr. Woodard:

Deseo expresarle mi agradecimiento por su ayuda para que mi hijo Javier pueda estudiar el grado 12 en su escuela el próximo año escolar.

Estoy seguro que Javier se adaptará perfectamente a la escuela y creo que será un buen embajador español lo cual será demostrado por los resultados de sus estudios, a pesar del problema del idioma que tendrá al principio, —pero que lo superará con buena calificación.

Me comunica la Embajada de los Estados Unidos que necesitamos la aplicación FY-20 del Estado firmada y autorizada por el Colegio para poder realizar los trámites de visado y permanencia allí durante un año.

Con mi reconocimiento por todo ello, le saluda atentamente.

Javier Montoya

23 According to this letter, what is Mr. Montoya's son going to do?

1 work for the Spanish Embassy in the United States
2 study in the United States for one year
3 improve his English before coming to the United States
4 move permanently to the United States

Gracias por esta linda revista, e informativa, ya que tiene de todo un poco y para todos los gustos. El motivo por el que les estoy escribiendo es que la revista No.14 no me ha llegado. Como podrán saber, mi correspondencia llega a una caja en el correo y yo no tengo problemas de que se me pierda. Por favor, ¿pudieran enviarme ese ejemplar No.14, ya que nunca lo recibí? También quiero pedirles que escriban algo del cantante argentino Sandro. ¿Qué ha sido de él en estos años?

—Alicia E. Mastrangelo
Los Angeles, CA, EE.UU.

24 Why did Alicia write to this magazine?

1 to contact a pen pal
2 to request a back issue
3 to answer an advertisement
4 to renew a subscription

ANUNCIOS
SOY UNA FRANCESA
de 19 años y después de las vacaciones vendré a estudiar en la universidad de Cádiz. Ya que no conozco a nadie en esta provincia, busco amigos y amigas con quines cartearme. Si eres de Cádiz o incluso de otra región, escríbeme. Te contestaré. Y luego, nos podremos encontrar personalmente y hacernos grandes amigos. Sigrid Beaupain. 149 rue du Fort. 59330 Hautmont, Francia.

25 What is this person looking for?

1 people with whom she could study Spanish
2 information about foreign study
3 someone with whom to correspond
4 a friend with whom she has lost contact

(c) **Directions** (26–30): In the following passage there are five blank spaces numbered 26 through 30. Each blank space represents a missing word or expression. For each blank space, four possible completions are provided. Only one of them makes sense *in the context of the passage*.

First, read the passage in its entirety to determine its general meaning. Then read it a second time. For each blank space, choose the completion that makes the best sense and write its *number* in the space provided on your answer sheet. [10]

Antonio Banderas

Antonio Banderas nació en Málaga, España, en 1960, y se interesó por la actuación desde muy pequeño. Pero al ver en un escenario el musical *Hair*, Banderas decidió seguir una carrera artística. "Quiero hacer lo mismo que esta gente", se dijo. Era tal la energía que demostraban los ___(26)____ de la obra musical, tan moderno el espectáculo y los colores, que Banderas dio el paso. Al día siguiente creó su propio grupo dramático.

Durante cinco años hizo teatro clásico, estudió en la escuela de arte dramático, hizo teatro experimental hasta que se fue a Madrid porque estaba aburrido. Allí tenía un amigo argentino que le ofreció el sofá para que durmiera. Pasó seis meses en aquella casa, durmiendo en el sofá. Luego consiguió un trabajo y se mudó. En dos años en Madrid, Antonio ___(27)____ en once casas. Hubo ocasiones en que ni siquiera deshizo la maleta.

Un amigo de Antonio le dijo que él conocía a un director de cine que tal vez lo podía ayudar. Fue entonces cuando conoció a Pedro Almodóvar. Almodóvar fue a ver una función en la que trabajaba Antonio y le dijo: "¡Oye! ¿Quieres hacer una ___(28)____ conmigo? Es un papelito corto que te puede interesar". Antonio dijo que sí, y así comenzó una relación de trabajo que duró por siete años.

Antonio hace el "crossover" al cine norteamericano con la película "The Mambo Kings", que es la historia de dos hermanos cubanos que vienen en busca del sueño americano. Con esta película Banderas despertó mucho entusiasmo y se le consideró un amante latino. "Me imagino que eso ocurrió porque tengo el cabello oscuro y están buscando a un nuevo actor romántico como Rodolfo Valentino", dijo él.

En la actualidad, Hollywood mantiene a Banderas muy ___(29)___. Y por eso él trabaja mucho. Una de sus películas, "Desperado", tiene lugar en una población mexicana. Antonio se muestra capaz de ingresar a la liga de los héroes de acción y con un toque latino.

El actor asumió el dasafío más grande de su carrera al participar en la famosa película "Evita". Esta película es la versión cinematográfica del musical del mismo ___(30)___ creado por el compositor Andrew Lloyd Webber. La película, a un costo de 40 millones de dólares, fue dirigida por Alan Parker. Madonna interpretó a Eva Perón y Banderas a Ché Guevara. A Antonio Banderas le gustaría seguir trabajando en los Estados Unidos, un país que según él facilita el crecimiento de los artistas ue tienen talento. "Esto está clarísimo. Es una lección que ya me aprendí".

(26) 1 jugadores
      2 actores
      3 productores
      4 traductores

(27) 1 cantó
      2 actuó
      3 vivió
      4 estudió

(28) 1 película
      2 canción
      3 escuela
      4 investigación

(29) 1 desilusionado
      2 aburrido
      3 triste
      4 ocupado

(30) 1 título
      2 estado
      3 horario
      4 concurso

PART 3

Write your answers to Part 3 according to the directions for *a* and *b*. [16]

(*a*) *Directions:* In your answer booklet, write **one** well-organized note in Spanish as directed below. [6]

Choose **either** question 31 **or** 32. Write the number of the question you have chosen in the space provided on your answer sheet. Write a well-organized note, following the specific instructions given in the question you have chosen. Your note must consist of **at least six clauses**. To qualify for credit, a clause must contain a verb, a stated or implied subject, and additional words necessary to convey meaning. The six clauses may be contained in fewer than six sentences if some of the sentences have more than one clause.

---

31 The host mother of a Spanish exchange student in your school is having a birthday. The student does not know what to buy for her and is looking for suggestions. Write a note in Spanish to the exchange student an appropriate present.

In your note, you may wish to mention why the present you suggest is appropriate, where the student can buy the present, approximately how much it will cost, and your willingness to help the student shop. **Be sure to accomplish the purpose of the note, which is *to suggest an appropriate present.***

Use the following:

   Salutation: [exchange student's first name]
   Closing: [your name]

The salutation and closing will *not* be counted as part of the six required clauses.

32 Your Spanish teacher has given your class a homework assignment that is due tomorrow. However, you will be unable to complete it by then and want to request a time extension. In Spanish, write a note to your Spanish teacher requesting a time extension on this homework assignment.

In the note, you may wish to include the reason for the request (e.g., what you have to do tonight, why completing the homework is not possible), the amount of time you need, and what you are going to do to complete the assignment (e.g., work in the library, read more books, rewrite material). You may also wish to express your appreciation to your teacher for considering your request. **Be sure to accomplish the purpose of the note, which is *to request a time extension on the homework assignment.***

Use the following:

Salutation: Sr./ Sra. [your teacher's name]

Closing: [your name]

The salutation and closing will not be counted as part of the six required clauses.

Directions: On your answer sheet, write **one** well-organized composition in Spanish as directed below. [10]

Choose **either** question 33 **or** 34. Write the number of the question you have chosen in the space provided on your answer sheet. Write a well-organized composition, following the specific instructions given in the question you have chosen. Your composition must consist of **at least 10 clauses**. To qualify for credit, a clause must contain a verb, a stated or implied subject, and additional words necessary to convey meaning. The 10 clauses may be contained in fewer than 10 sentences if some of the sentences have more than one clause.

---

33 In Spanish, write a story about the situation shown in the picture below. It must be a story relating to the picture, **not** a description of the picture. Do *not* write a dialogue.

34   You have just returned form a trip to Spain and have discovered that you left something in your host family's home. In Spanish, write a letter to your host family to request the return of the item.

You <u>must</u> accomplish the purpose of the letter, which is *to request the return of the item*.

In your letter, you may wish to mention how much you enjoyed your trip to Spain and staying at your host family's home. You may then want to mention that you left something at their home, describe the item, and explain why the item is important to you. You may want to suggest how the item should be returned to you and offer to pay for the expense. You may also wish to thank the family for their help in returning the item. You may use any or all of the ideas suggested above *or* you may use your own ideas. **Either way, you must request the return of the item.**

Use the following:

Dateline: el 22 de junio de 1999

Salutation: Querida Familia

Closing: Con cariño

The dateline, salutation, and closing will *not* be counted as part of the 10 required clauses.

LISTENING COMPREHENSION
PART 1A

Listening Comprehension: The following passages should be read aloud to the students during Part 1A. The background information should be read in English *once*, the passages should each be read in Spanish *twice*, and the question should be read in English *once*. Do not allow more than one minute between questions. [30]

---

1 You are an exchange student in a school in Chile. On the morning announcements, you hear:

Hay una reunión esta tarde a las tres y media para todos los que quieran participar en la primera producción dramática de la escuela. No es necesario tener experiencia. Lo más importante es tener interés en el teatro y el deseo de trabajar con nosotros.

What will take place this afternoon?

2 You hear this advertisement on a television program:

En épocas pasadas todas las niñas recibían una muñeca de regalo. Y era el juguete favorito de la niña. Hoy, sin embargo, los promovedores de muñecas tienen algo nuevo para las niñas, la muñeca clónica. Los padres mandan una foto de su hija a la compañía que fabrica las muñecas clónicas. Entonces, las muñecas son hechas a mano y las hacen parecidas a la persona en la foto. Algunos pediatras norteamericanos dicen que estas muñecas puedan ayudar a los niños.

What is required to purchase one of these dolls?

3 You are listening to the radio and hear this report:

Steven Fisher de los EEUU es especialista en lenguas del Pacífico. Es la primera persona que ha podido interpretar la misteriosa escritura jeroglífica de la isla chilena de Pascua. El señor Fisher mostró el texto escrito sobre tabla de madera. Esta escritura se basa en 120 pictogramas de criaturas y objetos. Cuando los pictogramas y los objetos se combinan, forman glifos o inscripciones. El señor Fisher pasó seis años visitando museos que poseen las tablas y descubrió la llave de los glifos en el Museo de Historia Natural de Santiago de Chile.

What did Steven Fisher discover?

4   While traveling in Costa Rica, you hear this announcement on the radio:

¡Viaja, hermano, para echar una mano! Cambiar las clásicas vacaciones en la playa por un viaje para ayudar a otros es una buena alternativa para este verano. Nuestra organización ofrece la posibilidad de cuidar a enfermos, participar en programas de educación, de sanidad, de agricultura o limpieza medioambiental. Los participantes tendrán que tomar cursos para prepararse para todos los aspectos del viaje.

What does this advertisement offer?

5   You are in Santiago, Chile, and hear this news item:

En la ciudad, el señor Esmog está cada día más grande y poderoso. Señor Esmog crece con el humo negro y denso de los autos. Para combatir el esmog, las autoridades tienen una restricción de vehículos. De lunes a viernes, el último dígito de la matrícula determina cuándo se puede usar un auto. Por ejemplo, si es martes y el número termina en 6 o 0, hay que esperar hasta mañana para conducir su coche, o tiene que usar transporte público. Todos los días hay dos números diferentes y menos contaminación. ¡Pobre Esmog!

What information does the news report give?

6   After viewing a program at the planetarium, you hear this request:

Los voluntarios hacen muchos trabajos vitales en el Museo y el Planetario. Se emplean voluntarios en la tienda de regalos. También dan programas para estudiantes, ayudan con exhibiciones y eventos, o proveen seguridad para las funciones de laser y mucho más. Por favor, infórmese en la oficina si usted está interesado. ¡Nosotros lo necesitamos!

What kind of work are these volunteers expected to do?

7   You are at a hotel in Madrid, Spain, and you overhear the desk clerk talking to a newly arrived tourist. The desk clerk says:

Si Ud. desea cambiar sus dólares en pesetas lo puede realizar en muchos lugares. Los bancos están abiertos los días laborales de 8,30 a 14h., y los sabados de 9 a 13h. Casi todos los hoteles de 4 y 5 estrellas pueden cambiar su dinero igualmente que las agencias de viajes y los grandes almacenes. Si Ud. lo desea, nuestra caja aquí le puede ayudar con ese servicio. Estamos a sus órdenes.

What does the desk clerk explain to the tourist?

8   You hear this advertisement about a restaurant:

El restaurante "Mesónde Oro" debe ser el único en la ciudad que ofrece comidas en la piscina. Durante el invierno, tapan la piscina con una alfombra y se convierte en comedor. El resto del año, la descubren sólo con propósitos decorativos.

What is unusual about this restaurant?

9   You are an exchange student in Spain. You hear a lecturer discuss the origin of chess. He says:

El juego de ajedrez nació en India en el siglo VI. Los jugadores usaban cuatro peones, un rey, un barco y un elefante. El juego tenía las mismas reglas que una verdadera batalla. El objetivo de esta competencia era capturar al rey. De la India el juego pasó a Persia y después a Arabia. Los árabes introdujeron el juego en África del Norte y en España. Desde España, pasó a Europa, donde el barco y el elefante fueron sustituidos por la torre y el caballo.

According to this lecturer, where did the game of chess originate?

PART 1B

The following passages should be read aloud to the students during Part 1B. The background information should be read in English *once*, the passages should each be read in Spanish *twice* and the question should be read in Spanish *once*. Do not allow more than one minute between questions.

---

10   You are listening to a radio station in Puerto Rico and you hear this announcement:

"El gato negro" en Joyudas, Cabo Rojo, anuncia su apertura y lo celebra este sábado, primero de agosto, con una gran fiesta de inauguración. Para ayudar a celebrar el estreno de ste restaurante se presentarán al gran cantante de música salsa, Gilberto Santarosa y el grupo "Zona Roja". Tendremos disponible nuestro sabroso pollo asado, mariscos, empanadas de camarones, pescado y carne. ¡Les esperamos!

¿De qué se trata este anuncio?

11   You are with a tour group in Madrid and the tour guide says:

La Puerta del Sol, o solamente Sol, como la llaman los madrileños, es desde hace siglos el centro del Madrid popular. Es lugar de encuentro y de paso de muchos de los turistas y otros extranjeros que viajan a Madrid: unos se citan a la entrada del Metro, otros pasean, van de compras o simplemente, toman un refresco y observan a la gente desde un café.

¿Qué es la Puerta del Sol?

12   While touring Puerto Rico you hear this commentary by a tour guide:

En todas las Antillas, pocas ciudades muestran las etapas de su historian tan claramente como San Juan. A principios del siglo XVI, Juan Ponce de León estableció un pueblo que, en 1521, se convirtió en el Viejo San Juan. Hoy es uno de los mejores museos vivientes de arquitectura colonial, repleto de balcones de hierro y de calles de piedras. El fuerte de El Morro, al lado del mar, es un recuerdo del pasado militar.

A pocos pasos de la parte antigua de la ciudad brillan los hoteles modernos de la Playa del Condado. Hay numerosos casinos y espectáculos, y más allá, existen rascacielos y grandísimos centros comerciales en la parte nueva de la ciudad.

¿Qué dice el guía de la ciudad de San Juan?

13   While on a flight to Spain, you hear this announcement:

Con la confianza de ofrecerle lo mejor, Iberia ha seleccionado para usted 10 canales de audio donde podrá escoger desde los grandes músicos clásicos, hasta los últimos éxitos de las listas internacionales, así como música iberoamericana, japonesa…y mucho más. Para nuestros amigos más pequeños hemos dedicado un canal especial. Los auriculares para música le serán facilitados gratuitamente.

¿Qué se le ofrece al pasajero?

14   You are watching television in Barcelona, Spain, and you hear this announcement:

Pruebe Nueva Dermis, para rejuvenecer su piel sin cirugía. Nueva Dermis es un tratamiento moderno que renueva la piel, eliminando gradualmente las arrugas y las manchas de la vejez dando a la piel un nuevo tono joven y fresco. Además, Nueva Dermis es también un extraordinario tratamiento contra el acné y sus cicatrices, devolviendo al rostro un aspecto limpio y normal.

¿Qué es Nueva Dermis?

15   You are on an airplane that is landing at the airport in Mexico City and you hear this announcement:

El capitán y toda la tripulación espera que usted haya gozado de este vuelo con destino a la Ciudad de México. Y queremos recordarles que sus sugerencias y opiniones acerca de nuestro servicio son agradecidas. Queremos poder servirle mejor en el futuro.

En estos momentos nuerstras asistentes de vuelo les entregarán un corto cuestionario para que usted haga sus comentarios. Antes de desembarcar, deje el cuestionario en el asiento. Gracias por su cooperación.

En nombre de todo el personal de aviación les damos las gracias por volar con nosotros. Esperamos poder servirles pronto.

¿Qué información da este anuncio?

ANSWER BOOKLET
FOR
COMPREHENSIVE EXAMINATION
IN SPANISH

Student: .... Sex: ☐ Male ☐ Female

Teacher: ....

School: ....

City: ....

Part 1				
a 1..........	4..........	7..........	*b* 10..........	13..........
2..........	5..........	8..........	11..........	14..........
3..........	6..........	9..........	12..........	15..........

Credit

[a]

[OVER]

Part 2

	a			b			c	
	16			21			26	
	17			22			27	
	18			23			28	
	19			24			29	
	20			25			30	

Credit

Part 3a

Question Number _____

....

....

....

....

....

....

....

....

....

....

....

....

....

....

[b]

Part 3b

Question Number _____

....
....
....
....
....
....
....
....
....
....
....
....
....
....
....
....
....
....

Total Checks (4a + 4b): _____ /3 = Credit

[c]

Sample Test II Answers and Explanations

ANSWER KEY

1A	1B	2A	2B	2C
1. 4	10. 1	16. 1	21. 2	26. 2
2. 2	11. 3	17. 3	22. 4	27. 3
3. 3	12. 1	18. 4	23. 2	28. 1
4. 2	13. 2	19. 3	24. 2	29. 4
5. 1	14. 4	20. 2	25. 3	30. 1
6. 2	15. 1			
7. 3				
8. 4				
9. 4				

ANSWERS AND EXPLANATIONS
PART 1A

1 1 Although the announcement mentions a dramatic production (la producción dramática), it says nothing about a field trip or the local theater.
  2 The announcement does not mention basketball or tryouts.
  3 There is no mention of a presentation.
  4 "Hay una reunión…para todos los que quieran participar en la producción dramática de la escuela."

2 1 Toys are mentioned, but the advertisement is not specifically concerned with a toy that can be recycled.
  2 "Los padres mandan una foto de su hija."
  3 Although the passage mentions pediatricians, the ad deals with toys, not illnesses.
  4 The ad does not mention charitable contributions.

3 1 The radio report discusses the translation of some wooden tablets by an American language specialist. It does not say what purpose the tablets serve.
  2 The word languages (*lenguas*) is mentioned in the first sentence, but the focus of the report is on the fact that Steven Fisher has deciphered the meaning of the writing and hieroglyphics on these specific wooden tablets, not the importance of languages in general.
  3 "…que ha podido interpretar la misteriosa escritura jeroglífica…"
  4 Steven Fisher is the first person to translate these tablets. He is not the first person to inhabit Easter Island.

4 1 The advertisement asks people to change their vacation, not their career. Do not be misled because the activities the ad mentions sound more like work than vacation.
  2 "Cambiar las clásicas vacaciones en la playa por un viaje para ayudar a otros…"
  3 Traveling is mentioned prominently in the ad, but not in the context of travel rates.
  4 Participants have to take classes to prepare them for the trip, but Spanish classes are not mentioned specifically.

5   1   **"Para combatir el esmog, las autoridades tienen una restricción de vehículos."**

     2   Although smog is obviously bad for one's health, the news item does not mention the personal health dangers caused by smog.

     3   The news item mentions days of the week as it details an ongoing reduction plan, not because of any daily smog advisory.

     4   The news item does not mention the effect of smog on crops.

6   1   Volunteers are expected to perform a number of duties including presenting programs to students. Giving food to children is not mentioned in the list.

     2   **"Se emplean voluntarios en la tienda de regalos."**

3 & 4   Providing transportation to the office and helping with cleaning up are not mentioned in the list of volunteers' jobs.

7   1   You might be tempted to choose this answer because you are on vacation, but the clerk does not mention anything about your trip itinerary.

     2   The desk clerk gives the hours of operation for the banks in Madrid, not the hours of departure from the hotel.

     3   **"Si Ud. desea cambiar sus dólares en pesetas lo puede realizar en muchos lugares."**

     4   Four- and five-star hotels are mentioned only because they offer money-changing services.

8   1   The restaurant's hours of operation are not discussed.

     2   The passage does not mention exotic flowers.

     3   This would be a good guess if you had no idea what the correct answer was. However, the word *tapan* means "to cover." Do not confuse it with *tapas,* the word for Spanish appetizers or snacks.

     4   **"...que ofrece comidas en la piscina."**

9   1   The game was brought to Spain by the Arabs, but it did not originate there.

2 & 3   The passage says the game went from India to Persia and then to Arabia.

     4   **"El juego de ajedrez nació en India..."**

PART 1B

10 1 **"celebra este sábado, primero de agosto, con una gran fiesta de inauguración."**

      2 Only a singer and a group are mentioned, not two orchestras. Gilberto Santarosa is one man and "el grupo, 'Zona Roja'", is the group that will accompany him.

      3 Gilberto Santarosa is performing to celebrate the opening of the restaurant. There was no mention of a compact disc.

      4 Food will be served at the event, but the announcement focuses on the party, not the menu.

11

  1& 2 The *Puerta del Sol* is a well-known area in Madrid, but it has little to do with any dramatic work or a famous museum.

      3 **"La Puerta del Sol...es el centro del Madrid popular. Es lugar de encuentro y de paso..." The guide goes on to list a number of activities that people do in Puerta del Sol.**

      4 You should recognize that *Puerta del Sol* is a location, not a period in history.

12 1 **"...es uno de los mejores museos vivientes de arquitectura colonial...brillan los hoteles modernos...existen rascacielos y grandísimos centros comerciales..."**

      2 Ponce de Leon *established* the town in the sixteenth century.

      3 The tour guide speaks of modern hotels on Condado Beach.

      4 There are many modern buildings, but not *all* the buildings are modern. The first paragraph discusses the older buildings as well.

13 1 Many airlines offer travelers' magazines, however, this announcement does not mention magazines.

      2 **"10 canales de audio donde podrá escoger desde los grandes músicos clásicos...las listas internacionales, así como música iberoamericana, japonesa..."**

      3 The announcement says nothing about exercise.

      4 The announcement says there is a music channel for children, not a movie for kids.

14   1 *Nueva Dermis* changes the quality of your skin; it has nothing to do with what you eat.

      2 *Nueva Dermis* is a treatment, but it is for your skin not your hair.

      3 The ad does not mention a clinic.

      4 "Nueva Dermis es un tratamiento moderno que renueva la piel...es también un extrordinario tratamiento contra el acné..."

15   **1 "Y queremos recordarles que sus sugerencias y opiniones acerca de nuestro servicio son agredecidas."**

      2 The announcement does not indicate where the passengers should pick up their luggage.

      3 The announcement is concerned with better service, not new routes or better prices.

      4 You should have dismissed this choice from the start; Avianca is not even mentioned.

PART 2A

16   1 *Paragraph 1, lines 1–2*
       "Como muchos niños que se criaron en los años 50 y 60, Franklin Chang Díaz soñaba con ser astronauta."

17   3 *Paragraph 3, lines 2–4*
       "Chang Díaz, de 49 años, es el astronauta hispanoamericano más destacado de la NASA y el primer director latino del Laboratorio de Propulsión Avanzada de la NASA en Houston."

18   4 *Paragraph 4, line 1*
       "Luchar por sus sueños es parte de la tradición familiar de Chang Díaz."

19   3 *Paragraph 6, lines 3–5*
       "se ganó una beca de un año para empezar sus estudios en la Universidad de Connecticut. Esa ayuda económica era lo que yo necesitaba y de allí, mi carrera se encaminó."

20   2 *Paragraph 8, lines 2–4*
       "Ésa es la más importante porque reconoce las contribuciones de un inmigrante a los Estados Unidos."

PART 2B

21   1   Emanuel is a musician, not a painter.

      2   **"El internacional cantante mexicano Emanuel llegará el próximo 9 de octubre a la capital venezolana para promocionar su más reciente producción discográfica..."**

      3   The article details his promotional trip to Venezuela, not a world tour.

      4   The article does not say that he will play at an outdoor theater.

22   1   The overwhelming majority of words in the article have to do with food and cooking. You should have eliminated this answer choice form the start.

      2   The Olympic games are mentioned in the first paragraph, but only to describe the part of Barcelona where the restaurant is located.

      3   You might be tempted to choose this answer because of all the food-related vocabulary, but there is nothing else in the passage to lead you to believe the topic is a cooking class.

      4   **"el restaurante Talaia Mar...ofrece una de las mejores cocinas de Barcelona." If you couldn't get the answer from the passage, the title (Una de las grandes cocinas de Barcelona) should have given you a good clue.**

23   1   This is one of the more difficult questions on the exam. You might be tempted to select this answer, but if you look at the letter closely you'll see that Sr. Montoya refers to the *U.S.* Embassy, not the Spanish Embassy.

      2   **There are many clues in the letter, but no clear statement simply saying that the boy is going to study in the U.S. In the first paragraph Sr. Montoya thanks Mr. Woodard for his help in allowing his son to study at Mr. Woodard's school next year. Then he says that the boy will adapt well and be a good Spanish ambassador. The final clue is where Sr. Montoya says he needs to fill out some paperwork for the U.S. Embassy.**

      3   The boy has already improved his English.

      4   The boy will only be in the U.S. for twelfth grade.

24 1 There is no mention of Alicia trying to find a pen pal.

2 **"Por favor, ¿pudieran enviarme ese ejemplar No. 14, ya que nunca lo recibí?**

3 Alicia is writing to ask that they send her an issue of their magazine that she has not received. She is not answering any advertisement.

4 Though Alicia is familiar with the magazine and has many issues, she is writing to obtain one issue in particular, not to renew a subscription.

25 1 This is a tempting choice because she is a student, but she is looking for anyone from Cadiz where she will be attending school. She does not specifically state that she is looking for people with whom she can study.

2 Again she does mention school, but she is not looking for information about foreign study.

3 **"…busco amigos y amigas con quienes cartearme."**

4 She is looking for new friends, not old ones she's lost contact with.

PART 2C

26 2 The passage says that Banderas watched the musical *Hair* and decided *"Quiero hacer lo mismo que esta gente."* He wanted to be like the actors.

27 3 You were probably tempted to choose answer choice 2 (acted), but the sentences leading up to the blank describe places where Banderas lived. Also, the phrase following the blank (*en once casas*) means "in eleven houses," and thus should have tipped you off.

28 1 The passage describes Pedro Almodóvar as a film director (*un director de cine*) and he is the one offering Banderas a small role (*un papelito corto*).

29 4 The clue appears immediately after the blank. *Y por eso él trabaja mucho.* He works a lot; therefore, Banderas is very busy (*ocupado*).

30 1 The sentence containing the blank reads, "Evita, the film version of the musical of the same _____ created by the composer Andrew Lloyd Webber." Even if you didn't know what all the answer choices meant, *título* is so close to its English counterpart that you could have used process of elimination to pick the correct answer. The other choices *estado, horario,* and *concurso* do not make much sense.

PART 3A

31 Sample note:

Marta,

Yo sé que mañana es el cumpleaños de tu madre. Tengo una buen idea para su regalo./ Como ella es mujer de negocios,/ella puede usar una pluma elegante./ Puedes comprarla en la tienda cerca de escuela por veinte dólares./Podemos ir de compras mañana.

Ramón

32 Sample note:

Sr. Gonzalez,

Yo necesito más tiempo para hacer la tarea./ Esta noche tengo que ir al hospital/ para cuidar a mi abuela está enferma./ Yo haré la tarea en la biblioteca durante el fín de semana/ y yo se la daré el lunes.

Muchas gracias por considerar mi petición.

Mariano

PART 3B

33 Sample composition:

Para celebrar su aniversario de bodas/ el Sr. y la Sra. Rivera fueron al teatro./ Después comieron en su restaurante favorit, odonde tuvieron su primera cita./ Como ellos son clientes regulares,/ el dueño les dio un comedor privado./ También les dio el vino gratis./ El Sr. Rivera comió bistec/ y la Sra. Rivera comió camarones.

33 Sample composition:

el 22 de junio de 1999

Querida Familia,

He vuelto a Nueva York sin problema./ El viaje fue muy agradable./ Ya extraño a Barcelona/ y estoy pensando volver en el verano./ Su casa es muy comoda,/ gracias por su generosidad./ Olvidé traer mi album/ que contiene fotos de la ciudad y su familia./ Por favor envíenmela a Nueva York./ Claro, yo pagaré el franqueo.

Con cariño,

Marcos

Appendix

THEMATIC VOCABULARY

The following is a list of vocabulary covered in high school textbooks. Words are organized by meaning, rather than listed alphabetically.

Days of the week

All days of the week are masculine in Spanish.

Monday — lunes
Tuesday — martes
Wednesday — miércoles
Thursday — jueves
Friday — viernes
Saturday — sábado
Sunday — domingo

Months of the year

January — enero
February — febrero
March — marzo
April — abril
May — mayo
June — junio
July — julio
August — agosto
September — septiembre
October — octubre
November — noviembre
December — diciembre

The seasons of the year

spring — primavera
summer — verano
autumm — otoño
winter — invierno

At the airport

agent — agente
arrival — llegada
available — disponible
board, go aboard — embarcarse
boarding gate — puerta de embarque
boarding past — tarjeta de embarque
change planes — cambiar de avión
check (luggage) — facturar (el equipaje)
counter — mostrador
customs agent — aduanero
customs declaration — declaración de
  aduana
declare — declarar
departure — salida
destination — destino
fare — tarifa
fasten the seat belt — abrocharse el
  cinturón de seguridad
first class — primera clase
flight attendant — asistente de vuelo
flight — vuelo
fly — volar
full — lleno, completo
label, tag — etiqueta
land — aterrizar
luggage — equipaje
make a line — hacer la cola
nonstop — sin escala
on the aisle — en el pasillo
passport — pasaporte

passenger — pasajero
personal belongings — efectos
personales
row — fila
seat — asiento
security check — control de seguridad
stop — escala
suitcase — maleta
to take off — despegar
terminal — terminal
ticket — boleto
tourist card — tarjeta de turista
visa — visa

At the restaurant

Appetizers — entremeses
check — cuenta
dessert — postre
fish — pescado
fried — frito
fruit — fruta
house specialty — especialidad de la casa
main course — plato principal
meat — carne
menu — menú
salad — ensalada
soup — sopa
tip — propina
vegetables — vegetales — m, legumbres
waiter — camarero
waitress — camarera

At the hotel

air conditioning — aire acondicionado
available — disponible
bath — baño
bed — cama
bellhop — botones

cashier — cajero
clerk — recepcionista (m&f)
elevator — ascensor
full — lleno
guest — huésped
heat — calefacción
key — lave
registration — recepción
reservation — reservación, reserva
room service — servicio de cuartos, (habitaciones)
room — cuarto — habitación
swimming pool — piscina

At the Clothing Store

to be in style — estar de moda
belt — cinturón
blouse — blusa
coat — abrigo, sobretodo
cap — gorra, gorro
dress — vestido
fabric — tela
glove — guante
handkerchief — pañuelo
hat — sombrero
jacket — chaqueta
match — hacer juego con
measure — medir
pants — pantalones
pay cash — pagar al contado, en efectivo
pocketbook — bolso, bolsa
raincoat — impermeable
scarf — bufanda
shirt — camisa
size — talla
skirt — falda
sock — calcetín
stocking — media

suit — traje
sweater — suéter
swimsuit — traje de baño
t-shirt — camiseta
tie — corbata

In the shoe store

boot — bota
fit — quedarle bien, bad fit — quedarle mal
heel — tacón
high heel — tacones altos
leather — cuero
measure — medir
narrow — estrecho
pair — par
sandal — sandalia
shoe — zapato
shoelaces — cordones
size — numero
sneakers — zapatos de tenis
sole — suela
vest — chaleco
wide — ancho

In the doctor's office

ache — dolor
bandage — vendaje, venda
break — romperse (+part of the body)
chill — escalofrío
cold — catarro, resfriado
cough — tos
dizzy — mareado
ear — oido
earache — dolor de oído
fiber — fiebre
flu — gripe
headache — dolor de cabeza
hurt — tener dolor de...

injection — inyección
sick — enfermo
sneeze — estornudar
sore throat — dolor de garganta
stomach ache — dolor de estomago
symptom — síntoma
to cough — toser
weigh — pesar

At the food store

bakery — panadería
butcher shop — carnicería
fish store — pescadería
grocery store — bodega
market — mercado
supermarket — supermercado

In school

attend — asistir a
backpack — mochila
ballpoint pen — bolígrafo
book — libro
chalkboard — pizarra
classroom — aula, salón de clases
desk — pupitre
elementary school — escuela
fail — salir mal, ser suspendido
get good (bad) grades — sacar buenas
  (malas) notas
grade — nota
graduate — graduarse
high school — escuela secundaria
homework — tarea
learn — aprender
lesson — lección
major (in), specialize (in) — especializarse
notebook — cuaderno
pass — salir bien, aprobar
pencil — lápiz

principal — director, directora
register — matricularse
report — informe
schedule — horario
scholarship — beca
student — estudiante, alumno
subject — asignatura
take notes — tomar apuntes
teach — enseñar
teacher — maestro
test — examen

In the movie house/theater

act — acto
actor — actor
actress — actriz
be about — tratarse de
box office — taquilla
character — personaje
comedy — comedia
drama — drama
stage, scenery — escenario
musical — obra musical
performance — función
play a roll — hacer el papel de
plot — drama
row — fila
scene — escena
screen — pantalla
seat — asiento
ticket — entrada
tragedy — tragedia
work — obra

In the bank

acount — cuenta
bill — billete
borrow — pedir prestado
cash — dinero en efectivo
change (loose coins) — suelto, cambio

check — cheque
checking account — cuenta de cheque, cuenta corriente
coin — moneda
credit card — tarjeta de crédito
deposit — depositar, hacer un deposito
exchange — cambiar
loan — préstamo
money — dinero
save — ahorrar
savings account — cuenta de ahorro
to cash — cobrar
traveler's check — cheque de viajero
withdraw — sacar

In the post office

address — dirección
air mail — correo aéreo
deliver — repartir
letter — carta
mail carrier — cartero
mailbox — buzón
money order — giro postal
package — paquete
post office box — apartado postal

Using the telephone

area code — código de área
busy — ocupado
call — llamada
collect call — llamada con cobro revertido
dial tone — tono, señal
dial — marcar
hand up — colgar
local — local
long distance — larga distancia
message — mensaje
number — numero
operator — operador, telefonista

person to person — de persona a persona
pick up — descolgar, responder
ring — sonar
telephone book — guía telefónica
telephone booth — cabina telefónica
wrong number — número equivocado

Sports

ball — balón (soccer)
ball — pelota, (baseball, tennis, etc.)
baseball — béisbol
basket — canasta, cesto
basketball — baloncesto, basquetbol
court — cancha
football — fútbol americano
lose — perder
match — partido
net — red
play — jugar
player — jugador, jugadora
racket — raqueta
referee — arbitro
soccer — fútbol
sprain — torcerse
team — equipo
tennis — tenis
throw — lanzar
tournament — torneo
train — entrenar (se)
volleyball — volibol
win — ganar

Means of transportation

arrival — llegada
brake — frenar
bus — autobús
delay — demora
departure — salida

destination — destino
early — adelantado
express — expreso
gas — gasolina
horn — bocina
late — con retraso, atrasado
license — permiso de conducir
lugagge — equipaje
on time — a tiempo
one way — sencillo
platform — anden
rent — alquilar
reserved — reservado
ride a bike — montar una bicicleta
ride a horse — montar un caballo
round trip — viaje de ida y de vuelta
schedule — horario
start (a motor) — arrancar
start the car — poner el coche en marcha
station — estación
stop — parar
postcard — tarjeta postal
send — enviar, mandar
sender — remitente
shipping charge — costo de envío
stamp — estampilla, sello
telegram — telegrama
window — ventanilla
zip code — zona postal

At the hairdresser/barber

beard — barba
cut — cortar
dye — teñir
haircut — corte de pelo
hairdresser — barbero, peluquero

manicure — manicura
moustache — bigote
pedicure — pedicura
shampoo — champú
shave — afeitar
sideburn — patilla
trim — recorte

Animals, insects, etc.

ant — hormiga
bear — oso
bee — abeja
bull — toro
butterfly — mariposa
camel — camello
cat — gato
chicken — pollo
cow — vaca
deer — venado
dog — perro
dolphin — delfín
donkey — burro
duck — pato
eagle — águila
elephant — elefante
fish — pez (live), pescado
fly — mosca
fox — zorro
frog — rana
giraffe — jirafa
goat — cabra
hen — gallina
horse — caballo
lamb — oveja
lion — león
mare — yegua

mosquito — mosquito
mouse — ratón
parakeet — perico
pig — cerdo
rabbit — conejo
rat — rata
roach — cucaracha
rooster — gallo
serpent — serpiente
spider — araña
squirrel — ardilla
tiger — tigre
turtle — tortuga
whale — ballena
wolf — lobo
zebra — cebra

Professions and occupations

All professions and occupations appear in the masculine form first and then the feminine.

accountant — contador, contadora
actor — actor, actriz
announcer — locutor, locutora
architect — arquitecto, arquitecta
astronaut — astronauta
author — autor, autora
baker — panadero, panadera
barber — barbero
businessman — hombre de negocios
businesswoman — mujer de negocios
butcher — carnicero, carnicera
carpenter — carpintero, carpintera
dentist — dentista
doctor — médico, doctor; médica, doctora
driver — conductor, conductora

engineer — ingeniero, ingeniera
flight attendant — asistente de vuelo
hairdresser — peluquero, peluquera
house wife — ama de casa
journalist — reportero, reportera
lawyer — abogado, abogada
mechanic — mecánico, mecánica
nurse — enfermero, enfermera
photographer — fotógrafo, fotógrafa
programmer — programador, programadora
salesperson — vendedor, vendedora
secretary — secretario, secretaria
shoemaker — zapatero, zapatera
singer — cantante
surgeon — cirujano, cirujana
taxi driver — taxista
teacher — maestro, profesor, maestra, profesora
waiter — camarero, camarera
writer — escritor, escritora

Countries and nationalities

Spanish-speaking Countries

Argentina — argentino/a
Bolivia — boliviano/a
Colombia — colombiano/a
Chile — chileno/a
Costa Rica — costarricense/a
Cuba — cubano/a
Ecuador — ecuatoriano/a
El Salvador — salvadoreño/a
España — español/a
Guatemala — guatemalteco/a
Honduras — hondureño/a
México — mexicano/a
Nicaragua — nicaragüense/a

Panamá—panameño/a
Paraguay—paraguayo/a
Perú—peruano/a
Puerto Rico—puertorriqueño/a
República Dominicana—dominicano/a
Uruguay—uruguayo/a
Venezuela—venezolano/a

Other countries

Alemania—alemán/a
Canadá—canadiense/a
China—chino/a
Corea—coreano/a
Haití—haitiano/a
India—indio/a
Inglaterra—inglés/a
Irlanda—irlandés/a
Italia—italiano/a
Japón—japonés/a
Filipinas—filipino/a
Portugal—portugués/a
Rusia—ruso/a

In the house

add—agregar, añadir
alarm clock—reloj, despertador
apron—delantal
armchair—sillón, butaca
balcony—balcón
bathtub—bañera
bed—cama
blanket—frazada, manta
boil—hervir
bookshelf—estante
burn—quemar
chair—silla
closet—armario
coffee table—mesita

cook—cocer, cocinar
cup—taza
desk—escritorios
dishwasher—lavaplatos
dresser—cómoda
faucet—grifo
food—comida, alimento
fork—tenedor
glass—vaso
hairdryer—secadora para el pelo
hanger—percha
iron—plancha (to iron—planchar)
kitchen range—estufa, cocina
knife—cuchillo
lamp—lampara
light—luz
meal—comida
microwave oven—horno de microondas
mirror—espejo
napkin—servilleta
night table—mesita de noche

Describing a person

Adjectives appear in the masculine form, unless otherwise noted. The feminine is formed by changing the -o to an -a. Adjectives that end in an -e or -i don't change.

To describe someone's appearance

big—grande
blonde—rubio
dark complected—moreno
elegant—elegante
fat—gordo, grueso
good-looking—guapo
poor—pobre
red-headed—pelirrojo
rich—rico

short — bajo
small — pequeño
strong — fuerte
tall — alto
thin — delgado, flaco
ugly — feo
weak — débil

To describe someone's personality or intelligence

boring — aburrido
careful — cuidadoso
clever — listo
courageous — valiente
cowardly — cobarde
crazy — loco
decisive — decisivo
diplomatic — diplomático
disobedient — desobediente
dumb — tonto
frank — franco
fun — divertido
generous — generoso
happy — alegre
hardworking — trabajador, trabajadora
honest — honesto, honrado
independent — independiente
intelligent — inteligente, listo
interesting — interesante
just — justo
kind — amable
lazy — perezoso
friendly — amistoso
nice — simpático
obedient — obediente
optimist — optimista
organized — organizado
pessimist — pesimista

respectful — respetuoso
romantic — romántico
sad — triste
sane — cuerdo
sarcastic — irónico/a
serious — serio
sincere — sincero
slow — lento
unpleasant — antipático

To describe physical or mental state

angry — enojado
anxious — ansioso
ashamed — avergonzado
busy — ocupado
calm — tranquilo
clean — limpio
depressed — deprimido
dirty — sucio
dry — seco
exhausted — agotado
furious — furioso
grateful — agradecido
happy — alegre, contento
healthy — saludable, sano
nervous — nervioso
relaxed — relajado
restless — inquieto
sad — triste
sick — enfermo
surprised — sorprendido
suspicious — sospechoso
tired — cansado
ungrateful — desagradecido
wet — mojado
worried — preocupado

Parts of the body

ankle — tobillo
arm — brazo
back — espalda
beard — barba
bladder — vejiga
blood — sangre
body — cuerpo
bone — hueso
brain — cerebro
calf — pantorrilla
cheek — mejilla
chest — pecho
chin — barbilla
dimple — hoyuelo
ear — oreja
elbow — codo
eye — ojo
eyebrow — ceja
eyelash — pestaña
eyelid — párpado
face — cara
features — rasgos
finger — dedo
fist — puño
foot — pie
forehead — frente
freckle — peca
hair — pelo, cabello
hand — mano
head — cabeza
heart — corazón
hip — cadera
inner ear — oído
jaw — mandíbula
kidney — riñón
knee — rodilla

leg — pierna
lip — labio
liver — hígado
lung — pulmón
moustache — bigote
mouth — boca
muscle — músculo
nail — una
neck — cuello
nose — nariz
shoulder — hombro
skeleton — esqueleto
skin — piel
thigh — muslo
throat — garganta
thumb — pulgar
tongue — lengua
vein — vena
waist — cintura
wisdom tooth — diente de juicio
wrist — muñeca

Numbers

Some points about numbers you can count on!

1. Numbers 16 through 19 and 21 through 29 can be written as three words:
   - *diez y seis, diez y siete, diez y ocho, diez y nueve, veinte y uno, veinte y dos, veinte y tres, veinte y cuatro, veinte y cinco, veinte y seis, veinte y siete, veinte y ocho, veinte y nueve* or as one word:
   - *dieciséis, diecisiete, dieciocho, diecinueve, veintiuno, veintidós, veintitrés, veinticuatro, veinticinco, veintiséis, veintisiete*

2. *Un* is not use before *cien (to)* and *mil*.

3. *Ciento* changes to *cien* when it is immediately in front of nouns, and in front of *mil* and *millones (de)*

   cien libros — a hundred books

   cien mil habitantes — one hundred thousand inhabitants

   cien millones de habitantes — one hundred million inhabitants

   In front of a feminine noun, *cientos* changes to — *cientas*

   Trescientos dolares — three-hundred dollars

   doscientas pesetas — two-hundred *pesetas*

4. Thousands are indicated with periods instead of commas in Spanish.

   1.000.000,00 = one million dollars and zero cents

Ordinal Numbers

first — primero, primera

second — segundo, segunda

third — tercero, tercera

fourth — cuarto, cuarta

fifth — quinto, quinta

sixth — sexto, sexta

seventh — séptimo, sétima

eighth — octavo, octava

ninth — noveno, novena

tenth — décimo, décima

Keep in mind the following when using ordinal numbers:

1. Ordinal numbers agree in gender and number with the nouns they modify.

2. *Quiero escuchar la primera canción.* I want to listen to the first song. Ordinal numbers may be placed in front of or after the noun. *El segundo párrafo está muy bien.* The second paragraph is very good.

3. In front of a masculine, singular noun *primero* and *tercero*, drop the final –o *José fue el primer presentador.* José was the first speaker. *Joaquín fue el tercer presentador.* Joaquin was the third speaker.

Cardinal numbers

All cardinal numbers are masculine in Spanish

0 cero

1 un (o), una

2 dos

3 tres

4 cuatro

5 cinco

6 seis

7 siete

8 ocho

9 nueve

10 diez

11 once

12 doce

13 trece

14 catorce

15 quince

16 dieciséis

17 diecisiete

18 dieciocho

19 diecinueve

20 veinte	100 cien (ciento)
21 veintiuno	101 ciento uno (una)
22 veintidós	102 ciento dos (tres, cuatro, etc.)
23 veintitrés	200 doscientos (as)
24 veinticuatro	300 trescientos (as)
25 veinticinco	400 cuatrocientos (as)
26 veintiséis	500 quinientos (as)
27 veintisiete	600 seiscientos (as)
28 veintiocho	700 setecientos (as)
29 veintinueve	800 ochocientos (as)
30 treinta	900 novecientos (as)
40 cuarenta	1,000 mil
50 cincuenta	2,000 dos mil (tres mil, cuatro mil)
60 sesenta	100,000 cien mil
70 setenta	200,000 doscientos (as) (mil)
80 ochenta	1,000,000 un millón (de+noun)
90 noventa	2,000,000 dos millones (de+noun)
	1,000,000,000 mil millones (de+noun)

ABOUT THE AUTHOR

Born in New Jersey to Cuban political refugees, Mr. Idavoy graduated from his home state's Drew University and Vermont's Middlebury College. He was recently hired as a permanent faculty member of Brookdale Community College's Modern Language Department in Lincroft, New Jersey. Mr. Idavoy also teaches Elementary Spanish and Language Pedagogy for New York University's School of Continuing and Professional Studies. He writes short stories and poems and is presently working on a first script. This is his first book.

NOTES

Expert Advice

Talk About It

Pop Surveys

Paying for it

THE
PRINCETON
REVIEW

Getting in

Word du Jour

Find-O-Rama School & Career Search

www.review.com

Best Schools

Finding it

FIND US...

International

Hong Kong
4/F Sun Hung Kai Centre
30 Harbour Road, Wan Chai,
Hong Kong
Tel: (011)85-2-517-3016

Japan
Fuji Building 40, 15-14
Sakuragaokacho, Shibuya Ku,
Tokyo 150, Japan
Tel: (011)81-3-3463-1343

Korea
Tae Young Bldg, 944-24,
Daechi- Dong, Kangnam-Ku
The Princeton Review- ANC
Seoul, Korea 135-280,
South Korea
Tel: (011)82-2-554-7763

Mexico City
PR Mex S De RL De Cv
Guanajuato 228 Col. Roma
06700 Mexico D.F., Mexico
Tel: 525-564-9468

Montreal
666 Sherbrooke St.
West, Suite 202
Montreal, QC H3A 1E7 Canada
Tel: (514) 499-0870

Pakistan
1 Bawa Park - 90 Upper Mall
Lahore, Pakistan
Tel: (011)92-42-571-2315

Spain
Pza. Castilla, 3 - 5° A, 28046
Madrid, Spain
Tel: (011)341-323-4212

Taiwan
155 Chung Hsiao East Road
Section 4 - 4th Floor,
Taipei R.O.C., Taiwan
Tel: (011)886-2-751-1243

Thailand
Building One, 99 Wireless Road
Bangkok, Thailand 10330
Tel: (662) 256-7080

Toronto
1240 Bay Street, Suite 300
Toronto M5R 2A7 Canada
Tel: (800) 495-7737
Tel: (716) 839-4391

Vancouver
4212 University Way NE,
Suite 204
Seattle, WA 98105
Tel: (206) 548-1100

National (U.S.)

We have over 60 offices around the U.S. and run courses in over 400 sites. For courses and locations within the U.S. call 1 (800) 2/Review and you will be routed to the nearest office.